MAINSTREAM *SPORT*

DANCIN' WITH SONNY LISTON

UP CLOSE AND PERSONAL WITH THE GREATEST NAMES IN SPORT

TOM CALLAHAN

MAINSTREAM
PUBLISHING
EDINBURGH AND LONDON

First published in Great Britain in 2004 by
MAINSTREAM PUBLISHING COMPANY (EDINBURGH) LTD
7 Albany Street
Edinburgh EH1 3UG

ISBN 1 84018 861 8

First published (under the title *The Bases Were Loaded (And So Was I)*) in the United States of America in 2004 by
Crown Publishers, New York
A division of Random House, Inc.

A catalogue record for this book is available from the
British Library

Typeset in Baskerville and Gill Sans Condensed

Printed and bound in Great Britain by
Cox & Wyman Ltd

DANCIN' WITH SONNY LISTON

ABOUT THE AUTHOR

Tom Callahan is a long-time observer of all sports, a former senior writer for *Time* magazine and columnist for the *Washington Post*. He is the author of *In Search of Tiger: A Journey Through Golf with Tiger Woods* and the co-author (with Dave Kindred) of *Around the World in 18 Holes*.

For John Leo, Roger Rosenblatt,
Stefan Kanfer, Lance Morrow,
R.Z. Sheppard and Paul Gray

ACKNOWLEDGEMENTS

Thanks to all of the gentlemen sportswriters, synonymous with their towns, who never failed to introduce the youngest writer to the manager. They loved newspapers more than sports and conversation more than dinner. I loved listening to them, especially Red Smith of New York, Jack Murphy of San Diego, Si Burick of Dayton, Blackie Sherrod of Dallas, Shirley Povich of Washington, Jim Murray and Mel Durslag of Los Angeles, Furman Bisher of Atlanta, Edwin Pope of Miami, Bill Gleason of Chicago, Fred Russell of Nashville, Tom Siler of Knoxville, Mike Barry of Louisville, Ray Fitzgerald of Boston, Bob Broeg of St Louis, Maury White of Des Moines, Roy McHugh of Pittsburgh, Frank Boggs of Oklahoma City, Milt Dunnell of Toronto, Bob August of Cleveland and Joe McGuff of Kansas City.

CONTENTS

PREFACE

Fedoras and Februarys

Long ago, when sportswriters were interesting people, Paul Gallico of the *New York Daily News* was as interesting as they came. While many of his press box companions were scarcely in charge of English, Gallico had complete command of French and German, too. He flew himself to assignments in his own airplane, making up to five stops per day. He would leave Bobby Jones at a golf tournament in Boston, swoop into Newport for the America's Cup, buzz by Belmont Park to cover the Futurity from the air, drop in on a late-afternoon polo match and end up at an evening fight. Gallico was a pioneer of participatory journalism, the original George Plimpton. For instance, Gallico boxed Jack Dempsey, who knocked him out in 1:37 of the first round. 'What's the matter, son?' Dempsey asked at the introductions. 'Don't your editors like you no more?'

Eventually deciding he wanted to try his hand at fiction, Gallico moved out of sports. Today, he wouldn't have to move out of sports to try his hand at fiction. But that's another story.

Actually, every sportswriter, if he gets around a little,

practises participatory journalism. It may be the boxer's or the golfer's story he is telling, but the places his stream crosses theirs are unique to him, and even the trestle he watches from is his own. Many tales have been told about the characters herein, and many more will be, but these are mine. You may know most of the players already, but you should be ready to meet at least a few of them all over again. My hope is that, fully assembled, all of the fragments and slivers will come together to form a full-length portrait of what Gallico called 'this geared-up, whirling, golden world'. My wish is that, along the way, you will be able to smell the cabbage.

I have endeavoured to stick to stories where I was at least as close to the subject as Henry Longhurst was to Douglas Bader, although occasionally I may have strayed as far away as Peter Dobereiner was from Longhurst. I'll try to explain.

Bader was a Second World War RAF flying ace who, even more than most of us (although just barely more than some of us), truly was the hero of all his stories. Both of his legs were lost slow-rolling a Bristol Bulldog at an air show. But Commander Bader was such a magnificent flier that a special Spitfire was outfitted for him and he proceeded to shoot down 30 Messerschmitts before colliding with one over France. Bailing out, he became separated from one of his tin legs on the glide down and was easily captured by the Germans. Sir Douglas was so highly esteemed, even by the enemy, that Britain was permitted to airdrop fresh prostheses, upon which he immediately escaped. Recaptured, he escaped again. In fact, he escaped so many times that the Germans ultimately took to confiscating Bader's legs each night and returning them to him in the morning.

Following the war, Bader attacked golf with the same obstinacy, whittling his handicap all the way down to four and becoming the closest of the many friends of the droll golf writer, broadcaster and raconteur, Longhurst, a Cambridge man and a former Member of Parliament, who lived in a windmill atop Sussex Downs.

In Longhurst's 70s, as poor Henry was melting away from cancer, Bader came to him every week with a bottle of gin and a tonic of fresh stories. 'Old friend,' Longhurst said at their final session, 'there's something I've always wondered.'

'What is it, Henry?' Bader replied.

'Will the grass be greener on the other side?'

Longhurst died that very week. Some months later, Bader emerged from a London taxi practically to trip over a beggar-woman in rags. As he fumbled for a coin, she said, 'I don't want your money. Are you Sir Douglas Bader?' He said that he was. Identifying herself as a clairvoyant, she said, 'I have a message from a friend of yours in the spirit world, name of Henry. I don't have his last name and I don't know what the message means. He said, "Tell Bader that the grass is greener on the other side."'

With that, she disappeared into the evening traffic. Sir Douglas was so unsettled that he got right back in the cab and went home. He never told anyone the story except Dobereiner, his friend – and mine. Peter suspected it was a hoax, prearranged by Longhurst, typical of Henry. Without any evidence, as usual, I disagreed. I think it *is* greener on the other side. This is also by way of fair warning that some of these stories are sentimental, and a number may seem to be fictions, but they aren't. Because they are sports stories, the great theme of my time-race – winds through them. As they are true stories, more than a few end in death.

In the vernacular of publishers, books dealing with a variety of subjects are termed 'collections'. Well, this is a collection of memories. Just to fix my place in the crowd, to explain how I happened to be standing there, I was an English major at Mount Saint Mary's College in Maryland, who never thought to ask what an English major does to make a living until the second semester of my senior year. I wasn't what you would call a born reporter. In 1963, I was sitting in a freshman Latin class when someone came pounding on the door, yelling, 'The President's been shot!' I thought he meant the president of Mount Saint Mary's. I wondered, 'Who'd shoot old Monsignor Kline?' Three years later, I volunteered to write an unpaid column for the weekly *Emmitsburg Chronicle* (one editor and a linotype machine), just for the clippings. This led to a writing job at the *Baltimore Evening Sun*, whose sports editor admired nothing about me so much as the fact that I had worked for free. I moved to the *San Diego Union* to cover the National Basketball Association and on to the *Cincinnati Enquirer* to write a sports column. Being 25 by then, I certainly knew more than enough to write a daily column. As a matter of fact, I knew everything. After I wrote ten years of columns there and at the *Washington Star*, the *Star* folded under me and I landed at *Time* magazine.

In almost ten years there, I wrote a lot of rancid stories and a few decent ones along with some thirty covers. I handled all of the sports for *Time*. Since then, at different times, I've written regularly for *US News & World Report*, *Newsweek* (just to complete a rare news-magazine Slam), the *Washington Post* and *Golf Digest*. I worked for *Newsweek* and the *Post* simultaneously. ('To be honest, I prefer *Time*,' I confessed to the *Post* editor, Ben Bradlee, 'but *Newsweek* owns a newspaper.' 'The hell they do!' he bellowed. 'We own them!')

Some of these stories, I've been telling and writing forever. In slightly different forms, the Secretariat, Cool Papa Bell and Arthur Ashe stories first appeared in the *Post*. My torrid love affair with actress Marilyn Maxwell was previously divulged in the book *Around the World in 18 Holes* (Dave Kindred, co-conspirator).

But it isn't entirely out of laziness that I am reprising assorted clumps. I just think it may be helpful to see a little of the work going on at the time. (Note Chapter Six.) The lion's share hasn't fit until now – everything fits eventually – and the main bodies are all fresh to the page. Cincinnati's Big Red Machine – the dominant baseball team of the mid-'70s – was still factory fresh when All-Star catcher Johnny Bench implied in his own book that I was involved with his wife. Finally, it is my turn at bat. Heads up, John.

'Miniatures' that fill the latter chapters are scatter-shot throughout the early ones. My colleague and friend, Art Spander, was bouncing along once in a car full of sportswriters bound for a Los Angeles Super Bowl, regaling them with another of his rapid-fire tales. Turning onto Santa Monica Boulevard, Art interrupted himself just long enough to shout – 'And there's the telephone pole that killed Ernie Kovacs!' – before blithely continuing on with his original story. Forgive us our press passes, that's the way we are. Incidentally, Art left out the smaller truth that, on the night the famed comedian died, Spander was a cub reporter working the overnight news desk for United Press International. Assigned to track down actress Edie Adams and to check out the bulletin that her husband had been in a car crash, Art actually succeeded in reaching her by telephone but then didn't have the heart to say why he was calling. He just left a message for Ernie.

I'm going to try to emphasise the smaller truths.

The route is the one suggested by the old fedora-wearing writer, Gallico, whose zigzagging flights from fights to Futurities just seems such a happy way to go. Years after he turned everything upside down with *The Poseidon Adventure*, and took up residence in an Irish castle, Gallico continued to hear the question: what made him leave sportswriting?

He always answered in a solitary word only an old sports columnist would instantly understand.

'February,' he said.

Here's to all the fedoras, and to all the Februarys.

I

Dancin' with Sonny Liston

Barry McGuigan was the featherweight champion of the world, a savage little boxer with enough going on inside his head to realise when there was less. He lost his title to a last-minute Mexican substitute, outdoors, on a 100-degree day in Las Vegas, 'a perfect cod of a town', in his Irish mother's perfect phrase.

When Barry was a young tough, he was carted like a carnival attraction from hill to hamlet through both Belfast and Dublin. 'They always put me on last,' he said, 'and I'd knock guys dead as Hector.'

This was more than just a figure of speech. He did kill a man, a Nigerian who fought under the name Young Ali.

'I still see that wee man in my dreams,' McGuigan said. 'Both of our wives were pregnant. He never knew it, but he had a son, too.'

A Catholic married to a Protestant, McGuigan lived so close to the boundary between Ireland and Ulster that he found it convenient to order his telephone from Northern Ireland and his electricity from the Republic. 'It's a fookin' joke,' he said. 'I stick my ferret in the ground in Clones and he goes in and out of fookin' Ireland all fookin' day long.'

When I asked him if he'd seen much of the Troubles, he laughed wearily. 'You mean, besides men with plastic bags over their heads and pitchforks in their hearts?'

McGuigan walked me to the car in the rain because he didn't want his wife to hear the final thing he had to say. It was raining hard. But he stood by the car and didn't hurry. Not even a week had passed since the title was lost, and not only the title.

'You know,' he whispered, 'I lost brain cells in that fight.'

'You sound fine to me,' I said.

'No, I've heard about this my whole life,' he said, 'and now I know what it is.'

On a training table in the Bahamas a week before his final fight, Muhammad Ali looked up and enquired, 'Are you 40 yet?'

Not yet.

With his left fist and his right index finger, he made a pantomime of lovemaking, in and out, in and out.

'After 40,' he said, 'it's not as good.'

'Does this mean you're down to five women a night?' I said.

Ali shook with laughter. Lord, how he could laugh. He was still himself then.

There were two halves of Ali. The first half was: 'Look at me, I'm so pretty; they can't touch me.' The second half was: 'They can hit me with everything; don't worry, I'm letting them do this.' The second half went on too long. Someday a pathologist will slice him open and scream.

In the first half, he was, as he said, bigger than boxing, a touchstone for racism, the Vietnam War and the 1960s themselves. During the assassination era, Ali was an overqualified candidate, yet he walked unprotected through the world.

Entertainer Steve Allen, everybody's pen pal, wrote in one of his letters that Ali was the only man or woman with whom he ever shared a stage who was quicker than Allen. He meant quicker to invention, quicker with the riff.

'You two are about the same height,' someone in the

audience noted. 'Who would win a fight between you two?'

Ali turned to the comedian, pursed his lips and blew. Allen fell over. On the way down, he thought, 'He initiated the riff.'

Ali was the actor. We all reacted to him.

As everyone knows, he could be incredibly animated. He could crack your eardrums. But, as you had to be around him a little to know, he could be just as awesomely lethargic. Long before the Parkinson's syndrome, long before the thickened Joe Louis head, Ali couldn't always summon the power to amplify.

Sitting beside him on a sofa, you might have to put your ear practically to his mouth to hear him. 'Champ, I can't hear you, Champ.' On the telephone sometimes, you had to fight to keep him awake. Other times, you couldn't get off the phone with him, even if the deadline was bearing down. You'd hand the receiver to your wife, write the story and come back into the room two hours later to find them still talking.

'How's Angie?' he'd say the next time you'd see him. 'I like her better than you.'

He was a beautiful and cruel fighter; the second part has been kindly forgotten. He was huge, bigger somehow than his cold dimensions. You had to stand beside him to realise how big he was. Or, better yet, stand beside Joe Bugner or some other giant he had been in the ring with, who hadn't seemed so large next to Ali.

Muhammad was good at blocking out the referee, great with his thumbs. He knew all the filthy little tricks of boxing and used them to torture Floyd Patterson and maim Ernie Terrell. There were occasional incidents of compassion. Trying to carry Chuck Wepner (the real Rocky Balboa) in Cleveland (not Philadelphia), Ali eventually turned to the writers at ringside and said with an exasperated sigh, 'I can't hold him up much longer.' The Bayonne Bleeder (not the Italian Stallion) fell of his own accord in the final round. Rocky didn't really go the distance.

At his cruellest after losing to Joe Frazier, Ali put on the glowing robe of 'The People's Champion', a gift of lights from Elvis Presley, and went about maligning apolitical old Joe in the black community. Muhammad called Frazier an Uncle Tom for visiting the White House, Ali's first stop on the way home from Zaire.

Zaire.

The celebrity writers – Norman Mailer ('He's the champ of fighters, I'm the champ of writers'), George Plimpton, Budd Schulberg, Hunter Thompson – stayed at the Memling Hotel or the InterContinental in the centre of Kinshasa, the old Léopoldville of the Belgian Congo. The working stiffs stayed at Mobutu's San Clemente Estate, N'Sele (pronounced Ensley), in the dusty boondocks. George Foreman took one look at the compound and moved into the InterContinental. Ali remained at N'Sele. That should have been the first clue.

While Ali ran up and down the hills from pagoda to pagoda, beautiful bribes from Red China to Mobutu, Foreman crossly walked his dog in the city. It is difficult now, in the light of his cheeseburger reincarnation, to recall how fearsome Foreman was then. Fighters who had been going the route with Ali and losing specious decisions were being knocked out of the ring by Foreman, who hit Frazier and Ken Norton like an iron ball hits a tenement.

George seemed happy that the African fight was at 4 a.m. 'I've had most of my fights at four in the morning,' he said menacingly. Since Foreman began fighting for purses without straps and little old ladies attached to them, he was 40 and 0. He was Mike Tyson and a half.

He was practically Sonny Liston.

Five years earlier, wearing a grey three-piece suit and a grey homburg, Liston got off a plane at the wrong airport, Dulles instead of Friendship, in a sour mood. He was coming to Baltimore to fight his chauffeur – well, not literally his chauffeur, but Amos 'Big Train' Lincoln, the next best thing. Geraldine, Sonny's wife with the gorgeous black curls, was along.

On the slow ride to Baltimore, Eddie Hricka, the matchmaker, drove. A young writer rode shotgun. Between them in the front seat sat the little bald trainer, Dick Sadler, a former song-and-dance man, graduate of the Our Gang comedies.

Sonny and Geraldine sat in the back as the writer tried to interview the former heavyweight champion of the world. First question. Sonny didn't answer. Second question. Sonny kept quiet.

'Please, Charles, please, Charles, please,' Geraldine whispered. Eventually, the writer gave up.

At the Belvedere Hotel, a tiny but fearless promoter named Eli Hanover poked his finger into Liston's stomach and told him it wouldn't hurt the gate if he would talk to the kid. Sonny grunted his assent and they went upstairs to a two-room suite. Leaving the others in the sitting room, Liston and the writer went into the bedroom and shut the door.

There, the game began anew. Sonny straddled a desk and the writer sat on one of two beds.

Question. No answer. Question. No answer. The writer started delivering the questions on automatic pilot, running down a bio sheet that Hanover had shoved into his hand on the way in. The writer's mind was elsewhere. He was thinking of the door.

Finally, he asked Liston, 'Can this be right? Are you only 36?' And Sonny leaped off the desk and grabbed him with both hands. Their noses were flattened on each other's faces. Very slowly, Liston said, 'Anyone who says I'm not 36 years old is calling my mother a liar.'

The writer put his face in Liston's chest and clutched two fistfuls of white shirt. Buttons flew off. Awkwardly, the Siamese twins banged about the room, knocking down pictures and lamps and sticking elbows into plaster walls. They fell over between the two beds and bounced right back up again, thanks entirely to Sonny's strength. No punches were thrown, but the clatter must have chilled the people in the sitting room.

It was Sadler who finally stuck his bald head in the door. 'W-w-what are you fellows doing in here?' he asked. 'Dancin'?'

'Yeah, yeah,' Sonny said, letting go. 'Dancin'.'

In the lobby bar of Kinshasa's Memling Hotel, Sadler (Foreman's man now) saw a face he hadn't seen in five years and broke into a little shim-sham-shimmy. 'Dancin',' he said, cackling and clapping and confusing almost everyone in the bar. 'Dancin' with Sonny Liston.'

The food at N'Sele was unsatisfactory: chickens that appeared to have been killed with hand grenades, gooey rib cages and yellow rice, and some kind of dark meat with teeth in it. At least Angelo Dundee found teeth in his. Dundee met the writers' charter from Paris at dawn. 'I'm so bored,' said Ali's trainer, 'I've been teaching the lizards push-ups.'

Led by Tshimpupu Em Tshimpupu, whose business card read 'Press Minister and Ring Announcer', the Zairois tried to be helpful in every way. The ushers at the Stade Du 20 Mai wore white painter's hats, which seemed appropriate to the photographers who had requested a darkroom and were delivered a room painted entirely black, ceiling and floor included.

The telex room was manned by operators fluent in Swahili, Lingala, Tshiluba and Kikonga but who spoke not one word of English. That made them ideal if slow typists, hunting and pecking, and seldom making a mistake. Because of the censors, it was advisable to end every piece with some variation of: 'And now I hand this to the censor of the great Mobutu Sese Seko, who is a marvellous host, beloved by the people in this estimable country, where the absence of petty criminals may be accounted for by the fact that they are sometimes hanged downtown.'

Almost all of the boxing people, who obviously had a stake in him, picked Ali. Almost all of the journalists were afraid for Ali. The precise breakdown was recorded on a legal yellow sheet (a betting pool, actually) tacked up on the wall of the American press agent Murray Goodman's hacienda at N'Sele. One night, Ali dropped in and ran his finger down the list. When he came to 'Foreman in 1', he looked around the room until he found the heretic and then crooked his finger. They went outside into the moonlight.

Hyacinths were floating down the Congo, renamed the Zaire, which in fact means 'river'. During the day, it was a brown, fetid cesspool. But at night it seemed romantic again. The clumps were mysterious shadow shapes on the water. The sounds of nearby birds and distant animals were somehow in tune and the African air tasted like rusty nails.

'I'm going to tell you something,' Ali said sort of seriously, without his usual burlesque, anyway, 'and I don't want you ever to forget it. Are you ready? Are you listening to me?

'Black men scare white men more than black men scare black men.'

The Twentieth of May Stadium rocked with 'Ali *bomaye* . . . Ali *bomaye*', Lingala for 'Ali kill him'. A giant portrait of Mobutu in his leopard cap looked down from the top of the stadium like Lenin at the revolution or the Camel smoker in New York City. Really, the President was watching on closed-circuit TV at the palace, where lions and tigers roamed free on the grounds.

Under the grandstands, in a tiny boiler room, a greying, balding Philadelphian sat in his underwear playing solitaire. He was Zack Clayton, the old Harlem Globetrotter. Zack was refereeing the fight. He looked up when two of us opened the wrong door and found him. 'Pray for me,' he said.

When the challenger came into the ring, he gleamed like a

copper kettle. Ali had raked his hair until every strand was just right. He looked magnificent.

Dundee was stuck in Foreman's corner, checking the gloves or something, as the interminable Zaire anthem began to play. Standing at attention right next to George, Angelo wasn't about to move.

'Angelo,' Ali called a couple of times across the ring, jerking his head for his trainer to cross over. Dundee stayed braced like a midshipman.

'Angelo, he's big!' Ali said as the anthem droned on. 'Look how big he is! Look at the arms on him, Angelo! He's huge! Look at him, Angelo!'

But, the funny thing was, Ali looked bigger.

When the bell sounded to end the first round, an active, concerned round for Ali, he raced to the corner, spat out his mouthpiece, and, looking over my shoulder at manager Herbert Muhammad, said, 'Leave him to me.' I turned to Vic Ziegel of the *New York Daily News* and said, 'Wrong again, Vic.'

During the rope-a-dope rounds, the celebrity writers first started a murmur of 'fix' and then, horrified for Ali's midsection, began to holler for the fight to be stopped. Ziegel gave me a look that said, 'These guys are idiots.'

It took a thousand punches to flatten George, but it *would* take that many. Ali had delicate hands. He sometimes bought a plane ticket for a greasy and lopsided heavy bag, the only one he ever found that he could bear to hit. Before fights, his knuckles were customarily shot with something like novocaine.

'Fooled you, fooled you, made fools of you, made fools of you all!' Ali sang, greeting the press bus returning to N'Sele. He had jogged all the way out to the entrance, more than a mile. And he was just beginning, beginning again. Manila would be even better, and far worse. Lots of Las Vegas was ahead. New Orleans.

His ultimate fight was always going to be in Tibet. Now and then he'd bring it up again with a lovely laugh. The morning after Leon Spinks whipped him in Vegas and left him to sleep in a bathtub full of ice, Ali sat uneasily in an easy chair in his hotel room, surrounded by a handful of the passengers who had so enjoyed his dizzying ride.

'I'm sorry, men,' he said finally from behind dark glasses. 'We never made it to Tibet.'

'Champ,' said Ed Schuyler of the Associated Press, 'with this guy, we'll be lucky to get to Scranton, Pennsylvania.'

Ali roared. God, how he could laugh.

With or without the title, Ali monopolised the spotlight. Shivering all his great lightweight career in the shade of Ali's shadow, overblown welterweight Roberto Duran finally came out into the half-light, as if from out of a cave, and was greeted by an Ali roughly his own size: Sugar Ray Leonard. Duran rubbed his eyes.

Later, he rubbed his stomach. When he quit during the rematch with Sugar Ray, a Leonard tour de force, nobody could believe either the alibi – the little wolf had wolfed down too much lunch – or the truth: the all-time uncivilised man had taken a civilised way out.

Between those fights, I went to Leonard's room at Caesars Palace to watch a baseball game with Ray and his brother, Harley. The return match had been announced in a Las Vegas ring the night before. Plumped out in his tuxedo, Duran looked like a gingerbread man.

Watching the ballgame, Leonard was in the process of analysing all the elements of the second fight (perfectly, as it turned out) when there was a knock on the door. It was Lola Falana, the showgirl. He introduced her, they had a few quiet words and she left.

As the game ended and I got up to go, Leonard said, 'Do me a favour, will you, big guy?'

'Sure.'

'Leave Lola out of the story.'

I picked Duran in the first fight. Watching the closing rounds in Montreal, I had thought to myself, 'Leonard will beat him next time.' But I was stubborn. I picked Duran again. I guess I loved Duran.

Before Leonard, Duran's archrival was a lethal lightweight named Esteban DeJesus. They fought three terrible wars, full of rabbit punches, butts, kicks, curses and low blows, their shared specialties. They were blood enemies.

DeJesus died of AIDS in prison. Close to the end, when Esteban weighed less than 90 pounds and no one was willing to touch him without rubber gloves, Duran burst into the ward and swatted away the offered gloves and mask to get to the bed. Lifting DeJesus into his bare arms, Duran rocked him like a baby and wept.

Duran and I had a minor relationship without words; that is, without English words. '*Maricón*,' he'd say, repeating Benny 'Kid' Paret's fatal insult to Emile Griffith. '*Numero uno*,' I'd reply. Or, if I saw Duran first, I'd say, '*Maricón*,' and he'd answer, '*Numero uno*.' I have no idea how this started.

On the morning after '*no más*', I stepped on the elevator at the Hyatt in New Orleans and there he was in a leather jacket and a faded green-and-white watchcap. A few handlers were along. Duran looked at me and shook his head slowly as if to say, 'Don't.'

I didn't.

A century later, Leonard and Duran would fight a third time, to no purpose. Wearing a blue watchcap in the corner between rounds, swaddled in a woollen blanket pinched off a bed at the Mirage hotel, Ray won a very cold decision on a very cold night.

Ali's coldest night was probably the night of the Larry Holmes fight in Las Vegas. By then, Muhammad had nothing to reply with, except his unblinking eyes. He didn't train for that fight, not really. He just reduced. He boiled the spinach, drank the juice and threw away the spinach. He dyed the grey flecks in his hair. He couldn't run from here to there, but he looked sensational.

'You pickin' me?' Ali said in his room.

'No, I'm picking the other guy,' I said.

'You always wrong.'

Later, at the door, I said, 'I won't mind being wrong,' and he smiled.

In the tenth round of a no-hitter, Ali turned sideways and dropped his face into his gloves, and at Herbert Muhammad's signal, Dundee stopped the fight. The aftermath was even worse.

That night, Ali's father, Cassius Marcellus Clay, was rolled by a prostitute, 'trick-rolled' in the charming phrase of the *Las Vegas Sun*. Imagine having a son like that, and watching him take a beating like that, and then going out and getting a prostitute.

From London, Joe Bugner telephoned Ali at the hotel and, in the upset of the evening, reached him.

'Joe, Joe,' Ali came on the phone to say, 'why are you calling me, Joe?'

'Because I wanted to make sure you were OK,' said Bugner, whose proudest accomplishment was that he twice went the distance with a pretty good Ali. 'Because I'm worried about you. Because I love you.'

'Joe,' Ali said, 'don't call me anymore. I'm not champ anymore. I'm nothin'.'

Bugner recalled his phone conversation with Ali as we ate dinner at the Canyon Hotel in Palm Springs, where he was helping Gerry Cooney prepare for Holmes. By this time, Ali had joined the cauliflower chorus paid to drop by camps and generate publicity, and then to attend the fights and be introduced in the ring.

'The old Ali,' Bugner said, 'would have come in today shouting, "This guy's an amateur and the other guy's my old sparring partner!" But he was like a beaten dog. I don't think it's just the punches, either. I think he's lost the pride he needs to be himself.'

Although England always thought Bugner was a Brit, and Australia still calls him 'Aussie Joe', he is, as a matter of fact, a Hungarian. Early on, Bugner killed a man in the ring. After that, typically, like Griffith, like most of the killers, he became a cutie-pie. Against Ali for 15 rounds and 12, he was a marble statue. But, in the gym with Cooney, he seemed fast.

'This young man has the greatest left hook I have ever felt – and that includes Frazier's,' Bugner said. 'He takes a good shot, Gerry does. He also delivers a bloody harder one.'

'Stop it, Joe,' I said. 'I'm losing respect for you.'

'You're right,' Bugner whispered. 'He's got no fuckin' chance.'

Standing 6 ft 6 in. tall, Cooney was a great big amiable man with a tiny little engaging voice. He was a huge hitter without huge hands, hatchet faced but handsome. Bent noses can be very becoming on fighters. Although Cooney could reasonably shave every four hours, either he was too busy for that at the Canyon Hotel or, as Holmes drew nearer, Gerry didn't trust himself around razors.

'You're worried for me,' Cooney said aside at a mass dinner one night. *Sports Illustrated* writer Bill Nack, *Time* photographer Neil Leifer and many others were there.

'I'm not worried,' I told him. 'I won't be in the ring with you.'

'Don't pay any attention to how I look in the gym,' he said. 'I never look good in the gym.'

Cooney and Sylvester Stallone shared a *Time* cover, if you can believe it. That was the cover that would have gagged a goat. It was a Leifer production. *Rocky III* was opening that week, and the brilliant little photographer had decided that Holmes just wasn't photogenic enough to remain champion. In Cooney's Las Vegas room the night before the fight, Leifer put the challenger on the telephone with Leifer's small son.

'Can I ask you a favour?' Cooney said to the boy, signing off in that little voice. 'Pray for me.'

'Ali never once said that,' I whispered to Leifer, 'and he was a minister.'

Cooney was a movie buff. We watched the Dudley Moore movie *Arthur* over and over in his room. During one showing, he gave me a haircut. Gerry hadn't studied on the Bowery, like the relief pitcher Tug McGraw. But he was pretty handy with the shears. In *Gentleman Jim*, Errol Flynn's old ode to Jim Corbett, Ward Bond portrayed both John L. Sullivan and Cooney's deceased father. Talking about his dad at breakfast, Cooney cried like a child.

I was Dirty Harry Callahan. 'You have to ask yourself one thing,' Cooney kept telling me in his best Clint Eastwood. '"Do I feel lucky?" Well, do you, punk?'

Cooney's trainer, Victor Valle, burst into the ring with about ten seconds left in the thirteenth round. He folded his arms around his fighter, pressing his head to Cooney's chest. They spun like a revolving lawn sprinkler. Gerry's left eyelid was sliced and the bridge of his two-tiered nose was split. He was badly beaten.

Into the ring microphone, Cooney said, 'I tried with all my heart. I love you. I'm sorry.' Holmes's cornerman, 82-year-old Ray Arcel, who once accompanied Ezzard Charles to a world championship, poked his sparrow head through the mob around Cooney's stool and whispered, 'Don't get discouraged, Gerry. Keep trying.'

I wrote the story and went to bed. In the middle of the night, *Time* called for a few more words. 'There are no pictures,' I was told.

How could that be? The fight, such as it was, went nearly 13 rounds.

Leifer wondered the same thing. He stormed into the office a day or so later demanding to know, 'Where was my take?'

'Neil,' he was told by a picture editor, 'you didn't have a take.'

To Leifer's credit, after dragging a magnifying glass over all of his many slides, he looked up and said, 'You're right. I didn't have a take.'

In every one of Neil's pictures, Cooney was hitting Holmes. As fast as he had to be shooting, with motorised cameras and all, I found that amazing. But it taught me something that I filed away for later. You can see only one man in a fight.

At the postfight press conference, Gerry mystified nearly everybody in the audience (all but one) when, in a quivering voice that could break a heart, he wound up his speech by saying, 'You have to ask yourself one thing: "Do I feel lucky?" Well, do you, punk?'

Bugner's take on Ali ('He's lost the pride to be himself') was as good as any. As the champ deteriorated into his palsy, the people who saw less in him and the people who saw more were both exaggerating.

At a lunch table in the Catskills, bracing himself for Tyson, Michael Spinks (Leon's smarter brother) told me his Ali story. Despite not really being a heavyweight, Michael beat – make that decisioned – Holmes twice. From across the ring before his first Holmes fight, Spinks studied the vacant figure of Ali, trundled in for ceremonial purposes. Ali's hands were at his sides and the fingers of one of them were jumping and popping and shaking pathetically. 'I was thinking how sad it was,' Spinks said. 'Then, suddenly, I realised what he was doing. He was telling me, "Stick, stick, stick, counterclockwise, stick, feint, move, clockwise, stick, stick, side to side." I nodded my head yes, and he stopped. That's how I started the fight against Holmes.'

Do softer sports have sweeter stories?

Several hours before Tyson won the championship against Trevor Berbick, colleague Dave Kindred led the way to Ali's hotel room, where we met Lonnie, Muhammad's new wife. Sonji, the first wife, had been smart and funny. After Ali joined the Nation of Islam and told her what to wear and where to walk, she told him a few things, too. Wife No. 2, Belinda, was a kid he met in a Muslim bakery. Veronica (No. 3) was a statuesque beauty, as large as he was large, in perfect proportion. There were a lot of demi-wives, too, and blizzards of children, all of whom he cherished.

But Lonnie was the most startling at first glance. She was red freckled and, with a little weight – a lot of weight – she would have been Odessa Clay, his mother.

For the millionth time, Ali performed his levitation trick and then reprised his entire magic act with the handkerchiefs, the pieces of rope and the rubber balls. Afterwards, in harmony with his religious beliefs, he gave away all of the mysteries. Then he sat down at a table to autograph a stack of sermons and listen to our conversation. On one of the sermons, he drew a little ring, and a little crowd, and two stick figures that he marked 'Ali' and 'Frazier'.

Berbick had been Muhammad's final opponent (a ten-round lost decision in the Bahamas, but they still couldn't knock him out). The rounds were started and stopped by the clanging of a cowbell. Not even Rod Serling would have written that. For us, Ali picked Berbick over Tyson. In doing so, it seemed to me, he was sort of picking himself.

The photographer Howard Bingham was in the hotel room. He is the only one of the 'entourage' who never took from Ali, who only gave. He and Kindred were talking about a white football player in Philadelphia who had just won an award over a black one.

'He had the complexion,' I said, 'to make the connection.'

★DANCIN' WITH SONNY LISTON

Ali looked up from his sermons as if he had never heard that before, or as if he *had* heard it, somewhere. He laughed slightly. That great laugh was gone.

He had tried acting. He had tried diplomacy. ('The black Henry Kissinger!') Ali never cared for the pain of boxing. He hated being left in the ice while everyone else went to the dance. In his heart, he retired after every hard fight.

But he never could find anything else in which to be 'the greatest of all times'. Nothing but boxing brought him poetry. 'Me', went his briefest and most profound poem, 'Whee'. So, he stayed too long.

When Ali staggered away in a haze of L-dopa, the game continued on. Leonard upset Marvin Hagler because black men scare white men more than black men scare black men. And, because you can only watch one man in a fight, from the sixth round on, everyone was watching Leonard, wondering why he was still there. Subsequently, Sugar Ray took up golf. Mike Tyson became the sport's central figure.

As a fictional character, Tyson would have been an offence to everyone, a stereotype wrung out past infinity to obscenity. His literary pedigree was by Charles Dickens out of Budd Schulberg. When Tyson, the juvenile delinquent, wasn't mugging and robbing, he actually raised pigeons in a rooftop coop, exactly like *On the Waterfront*'s Terry Malloy. Here was the black Brooklyn street thug from reform school, adopted by the white benevolent old character from the country, who could only imagine the terrible violence done to the boy from the terrible violence the boy could do to others. Agents of guardian-manager Cus D'Amato found Tyson handcuffed to a radiator in the Bad Boys' cabin. Turning pro the year of Cus's death, Tyson knocked out eighteen men for a start, twelve of them within three minutes, six of those within sixty seconds. He did not jab them; he mauled them with both hands. They fell in sections. As soon as Tyson possessed all of the many heavyweight belts, fuzzy-wigged promoter Don King threw a coronation for history's youngest heavyweight champion. (The boardwalk age-guessers would have been lucky to pick his century, but he truly was only 21.)

It was a melancholy scene right out of *King Kong*. Tyson was crusted all over with what the promoter called 'baubles, rubies and fabulous other doodads'. Ali crowned him. Beholding the dull eyes and meek surprise under the lopsided crown and chinchilla cloak, King said he was reminded 'of Homer's Odysseus returning to Ithaca to gather his dissembled fiefdoms'. With a pathetic sigh, Tyson said, 'It's tough being the youngest anything.'

In dazzling order, Robin Givens took him for a husband; Buster Douglas batted him bubble-eyed; Evander Holyfield boxed his ears off; and Lennox Lewis stamped the period. After earning and spending some $300 million, Tyson declared bankruptcy. The odd thing was, with or without money or the title, in or out of the penitentiary, Tyson remained the image of boxing. He returned from his rape stretch tattooed with other men's faces: Mao Zedong and Arthur Ashe. Eventually he had his own face redrawn with swirling black icons, like Queequeg on the *Pequod*, and went around the edges of sanity threatening to eat children.

For the five minutes that Tyson appeared indestructible, people wondered how the best of Ali would have fared against him. This was silly. If you saw the two of them standing side-by-side, you'd laugh out loud. Furthermore, like all of D'Amato's fighters, Tyson boxed by the numbers. He was no Rembrandt. A 'one' was a left jab, a 'two' a left hook and so on.

From the corner, through a caved-in nose, trainer Kevin Rooney called out to Tyson, 'Seven-eight. Feint, two-one. Pick it up, six-one. There you go, seven-one. Now make it a six.

One, one, six, six, seven, one, six . . .'

By the second round, Ali would have known the numbers better than Tyson. He would have grinned like a safecracker awaiting just the right combination for everything to click open.

In his 50s, even as he looked so lost on television, sitting mute while others testified for him in Congress, Ali could still drive a car, though it took some faith to ride with him. Every time he started to cross the bumps in the middle of the highway, you'd nudge him a little and he'd cross back.

Bob Waters, *Newsday*'s longtime boxing writer, had just died. Bob was always one of Ali's favourites. Muhammad would sneak up behind Waters in the press room and kiss him on the top of his pink head.

'Champ, do you remember Bob Waters?'

'Vaguely,' said Ali at the wheel.

At least he remembered the word 'vaguely'. Sugar Ray Robinson forgot everything.

When the century awards floated down on Ali, like blossoms, he accepted them in his spacious tuxedo, the Olympic lamplighter with his hands aflutter, usually murmuring the same small joke about another comeback. The original diagnosis by Dr Dennis Cope of UCLA was Parkinson's syndrome (the symptoms without the disease) in alliance with pugilist's syndrome.

But, over time, journalists carelessly, or maybe wittingly, dropped the syndromes and just said Parkinson's disease. Those nearest to Ali encouraged the impression that the way he was now had little, perhaps even nothing, to do with boxing. Maybe this made them feel better.

Utterly unthreatening, absolutely innocent – Joe Louis-like, incredibly – he was finally the undisputed champion of everybody in the world. Carried along to 'peace missions' all over the globe, Ali went out as El Cid.

In the summer of 2003, 27 years after he purchased his dream place in Michigan, Ali was still walking the beloved Berrien Springs property near the lake. 'No people,' he said gratefully. 'Quiet.' Two or three times as Dave Kindred walked along with him, Dave had to reach out and grab Ali's arm to save him from falling. Muhammad's feet kept getting stuck in place and his upper body listed forward impatiently until the feet came around. Then, to rescue his balance, Ali had to take three, four or five quick little running steps to get rolling again. He was 61.

Down from 268 to 222 (thanks in part to a change in medication), Ali had grown a little salt-and-pepper moustache and looked fine. 'Dark Gable,' he said for Clark Gable, with an old glint in his eyes. Still, a wheelchair had to be just up ahead. 'Do you remember,' Dave asked me, 'how Ali had looked at Joe Louis in his chair in Las Vegas?'

The last time I saw Louis on his feet, he was refereeing a fight between Frazier and Jerry Quarry in New York. It was a day or two after Hale Irwin won the US Open at Winged Foot, which was the only reason I was in town. I studied Louis more than the two combatants. In a faded, brown-striped shirt, the Brown Bomber looked irrevocably lost in the ring. Certainly Quarry needed a hell of a lot more help than Louis could give him that night. The next time I saw Joe, he was in the cowboy hat and the chair at Caesars Palace, and Ali was looking on in horror.

In Rod Serling's teleplay *Requiem for a Heavyweight*, the young up-and-coming fighter who dispatches washed-up old Mountain McClintock is named Cassius Clay. On the way down, just like Louis, McClintock stops off in a wrestling ring. He is made to dance around the ring at the end, wearing an Indian headdress. Muhammad was spared that, at least.

Entering the now ghostly Berrien Springs gym, pulling on a pair of punching-bag gloves, Ali pushed the heavy bag away.

★DANCIN' WITH SONNY LISTON

The bag swayed and its chain creaked. He touched the bag softly with a left jab, bent his knees slightly, set his feet and threw a gentle right. Then, out of the past – wham! – he hooked it with a left. And – wham! – he doubled up powerfully. Wham! Wham! Wham! Wham!

He was home.

At the Ocean Apartments on the Atlantic City Boardwalk, the bookcase in the living room was essentially a prop. But it was stocked with real books. One of Mike Tyson's handlers plucked out *Plutarch's Lives* and began thumbing through it.

'Who wrote that?' Tyson asked eruditely. 'Rembrandt?'

(Rembrandt?)

'Plutarch wrote it,' I said.

Now he was pissed. Fuming, he paced up and down the apartment in his boxer shorts, the signal for his cornermen to run. The last time he was this agitated was when a wire service reporter had introduced himself as being from UPI.

'One of your trucks,' Tyson said, 'ran over my dog.'

Mike was thinking of UPS.

2

Heroes Have Very Short Lives

On a particularly shiny morning in Santa Monica, a friend, Christine, proposed a hike. She was breaking up with the actor Bill Bixby at the time. The beach house she was living in was his. Christine's walk necessitated a drive first, an intricate, serpentine spin up a mountain to a burned-out shell of a home that once belonged to the original Young Dr Kildare, Lew Ayres. Along the way, Christine was surprised when we came upon another car, a black Trans Am parked literally in the middle of nowhere. Inside it, John McEnroe was kissing a woman who was nearly as beautiful as Christine. As we inched by on the narrow trail, McEnroe looked left and saw the sportswriter through the two panes of glass. John didn't know exactly who the passerby was but recognised him as 'one of them'. He threw his arms up in a familiar display of disgust, as if to say, 'There's no place I can go where they aren't.' We just kept driving.

Playing tennis with a girl, and a younger girl at that, might have caused him the usual, expected, masculine, chauvinistic, Germanic amount of embarrassment, except for one thing. 'She could really hit it,' said Boris Becker, who smiled. He was the only German-German I'd ever met who enjoyed smiling. 'I was not as good as the good boys, so I had to practise with the good girls. She was the best girl.'

Recalling childhood rallies with Steffi Graf, Becker glowed like a lit pumpkin. 'Two kids,' he said, 'from the same little area [the neighbouring towns of Leimen and Bruehl, near Heidelberg], who practised together when they were nine and seven. Isn't it a little incredible?'

It was 1987. We were in Rome, in Becker's grand hotel suite. Ion Tiriac, the Rumanian Rasputin who had taken charge of Becker and was introducing him to life, adamantly restricted all interviewing to the lobby, admitting only friends to the room. But, thanks to a lucky accident and Becker's great memory and good nature, Boris found a technical qualification for inviting me up. 'Pardon the mess,' he said. 'I live like a player.' He was 19. Before Tiriac left the lobby, he had said of Becker, 'Nobody has ever come so fast in the rankings to tenth, fifth, second, while his own generation of players is still hustling to get into tournaments. Is there another human being who gives 250 press conferences a year? There are six books out on him at the moment. In Germany, he is a god when he wins, a catastrophe when he loses. The pressure is inhuman.'

Tiriac's moustache bobbled as he spoke, like a spy's.

'Isn't he something?' Becker said in the room. 'He's learning me life. What other young men may ask their parents, I ask him. He has taught me everything – how to dress, how to handle women.'

As I was contemplating the dangers of learning women-handling from Tiriac, the doorknob in the adjoining room jiggled and someone slipped in quietly. Becker would have none of that.

He bounded into the bedroom and bounced back with his arm around a comely brunette named Benedicte Courtin. She was a Frenchwoman from Monaco, his tax haven. 'Boris Becker,' he trumpeted, sounding like a Frenchman, 'cannot love a woman?' Mademoiselle Courtin was 24.

Naturally, we started the conversation with Wimbledon. 'I was born there, you know,' he said. Two summers earlier, unseeded and 17, not to mention (in his estimation) 'very slow and very fat', Becker was basically assumed into heaven at Wimbledon.

'I didn't know what I was doing,' he said. 'In my mind, I was playing a little tennis tournament back in Leimen. Winning it again was more real. A little bit. I don't think a bad memory is possible for me there anymore. I can't promise I'll ever win there again, but I can promise I'll always enjoy being there. Years from now, I think I'll walk on to the property and smile.' Our chance meeting in 1985, which oddly he remembered, was a testament to what a rotten reporter I am. My family was along for that Wimbledon, and almost every morning the first week, we breakfasted at the Apple-Something Café around the corner from London's Gloucester Hotel. Since table space was scarce, we invited the big kid with the orange hair to sit down. He fell in with us three or four straight days. I never asked Becker a single question about the tournament.

One day, quarters were so tight that Don Budge had to call on a few of his old moves just to squeeze by our table. I told Budge, 'I just said to my wife that the greatest tennis player who ever lived is here, and she said, "Rod Laver?"'

Budge let out a howl. 'I like that,' he said. Boris looked hopelessly confused.

Faintly I knew Becker as a hard server who had broken his leg in Wimbledon's juniors the year before. Becker's English was slight. His manner was warm. I was astounded and delighted that he survived the first week of the fortnight. After that, of course, when the whole world wanted to ask him things, he vanished.

Every day, Henri Leconte or Tim Mayotte would come to the press room to say: Boris Becker is going to be a great player someday but he has no chance tomorrow. Until, finally, having won his own semi-final, Kevin Curren sat in the witness chair with one eye on a monitor showing just the cold numbers of the Anders Jarryd–Boris Becker semi. 'Go, Anders,' Curren mumbled. (Game, set, match.) Back then, Becker was a playful puppy with huge paws. Overnight, it seemed, he grew two or three inches to 6 ft 3 in. or 6 ft 4 in., and the peach fuzz changed to a pepper stubble.

'I have become an athlete,' he said in the hotel room, and he looked like an NBA swingman. 'I'm not Dr J., but I can dunk a basketball, just barely dunk it. Picking up a ball, any kind of ball, I always had a feeling for it. I knew how to handle it. I liked it.'

He could hardly express how much he loved tennis. 'But also I love to win,' he said. 'I can get better but I can't care any more than I do now. I'm very emotional on the court; my heart's in it, you know? I don't mean to throw myself on the ground all the time. It just comes.'

Late at night, 'under the cold sheets', he couldn't help wincing at his perpetually barked knees and elbows, and chuckling.

Vaulting the net after beating Jimmy Connors the week before, Becker had placed his arm about Connors's shoulders and positively dwarfed him. On critical points, in Connors style, baby Becker had been given to rearing up like a stallion in raucous celebrations. But Boris stopped doing this when he became the most powerful stud in the herd. It was unseemly.

The champion of a country, as Tiriac said, feels much more than athletic pressure. In West Germany, where headline writers were pleased to replace Bitburg with Becker, his name recognition was second to Volkswagen's and far ahead of Helmut Kohl's. The chancellor regarded Boris as a favourite grandchild. 'I came back from the White House one time,' Becker said, clapping his forehead at how preposterous that sounded, 'and sat up in bed and thought, "Hey, you were just talking with the most powerful man in the world. What's going on here? You're only a teenager."'

The Italian Open was going on but Becker wasn't playing in it. He was in Rome just to practise. The hotel had real clay courts, framed by amazing hanging gardens. That afternoon, Becker, Tiriac and a young sparring partner went out to hit.

'Do you know Germans?' Boris enquired as we walked.

'Just the stereotypes I see quadrennially at Olympic Games,' I said.

'Stereotypes?'

'Big-bottomed writers who look like U-boat commanders.'

His laughter rang through the courtyard.

'They never mind the queues,' I continued ridiculously. 'They're forever pushing their way to the front, bent on reminding the world why they have to have their asses kicked every 50 years.'

'While I practise,' Becker said, 'I'm going to think of the answer.' He worked a full two hours. I sat and watched him and also read an *International Herald Tribune* I had been lucky enough to scavenge in the lobby. Back at the room, Becker said, 'It's very, very difficult to be a German sometimes.'

'I was just kidding, Boris,' I said. 'Don't forget Beethoven and Marlene Dietrich.'

'I know, I know,' he said. 'But there *was* Nuremberg and there *is* guilt. It's silly to say about a tennis player, but I'm an unbelievable hero in Germany. And Germany needs heroes more than any place. Some of it, I don't care for. The eyes of some of the fans at Davis Cup matches scare me. There's no light in them. Fixed emotions. Blind worship. Horror. It makes me think of what happened to us long ago.

'And yet I want to be a hero, a small and good kind of hero, even though I know heroes have very short lives.'

Becker and Graf hadn't crossed paths in a while. My next stop was West Berlin to see her. But, from a distance, Boris's crystal set had been picking up friendly signals from Steffi.

'You can't imagine the pressure from the press back home,' he said. 'They've been playing us off in a little war, one against the other. But I can read the stories and tell how careful and generous she has been about it. She's a very kind person.'

As he walked me out, Becker said to pass along his best wishes to Steffi. 'Have you met the father?' he asked in a whisper.

'No.'

'Wait until you meet the father,' he said.

Billie Jean King's father, who was the same age as Bobby Riggs, 55, stayed on the outer edge of the tumult. 'Way to go, champ,' he said barely audibly.

'Thanks, Daddy,' Billie Jean called to him. 'That's my dad,' she said. Tennis's great Battle of the Sexes was over, and she and womankind had won.

Nora Ephron and Grace Lichtenstein couldn't keep their feet still. The women reporters all looked like they wanted to climb up into their heroine's lap. The whole rigmarole had begun the previous Mother's Day in Ramona, California, when Riggs presented Margaret Court with a bundle of flowers, and the winner of a record 24 Grand Slam titles promptly wilted.

There weren't very many reporters of either gender at the 'Mother's Day Massacre'. Neil Amdur was there for the *New York Times*. In a small grandstand at a little tennis club, Jack Murphy of the *San Diego Union* sat with his head down, reading leaked depositions in a bombshell lawsuit that former Charger lineman Houston Ridge was bringing against the National Football League. Every so often, Jack went, 'Whoa!' When he finally glanced up at the tennis, Riggs had won the first set, 6–2. In the next instant, Bobby had won the second, 6–1, and $20,000. The $300,000 Astrodome hustle was under way.

Riggs was a sad clown with fake cordovan hair who cheated at golf and life and married money over and over again and spent it. He found larceny amusing. At card tables and on golf courses, he liked being a chiseller. In golf, his chicanery included slathering the club faces of his irons with Vicks VapoRub. According to Bobby, this straightened the ball out a little. Riggs wasn't anywhere near the best of the over-50 tennis players. He couldn't have given ponytailed Torben Ulrich a game. But, thanks to his original coaches, Dr Esther Bartosh and Eleanor Tennant – two women – Riggs had been a wonderful player once.

In 1939, he was said to have parlayed $500 into $100,000 betting on himself to sweep the Wimbledon singles, doubles and mixed doubles, a trifecta never before accomplished. After doing it, Riggs won a few national championships. He barnstormed with Jack Kramer and played a lot of precooked exhibitions. Bobby was good at tennis but he was better at taking the price.

When the Big Top moved to Houston in September, Billie Jean worked and Riggs played. 'I am the one responsible for women's tennis,' she said. (Now others say it for her, and, of course, it is true.) 'I'm always the strong leader. For once I'm an underdog, and I love it.'

Among the characters hanging on to Riggs like pilot fish to a shark was a 'nutritional scientist' named Rheo Blair, who in an earlier age would have sold tonic out of a musical wagon. A few days before the extravaganza, Blair disclosed that the Riggs–King match had already been tried out on rats and that Bobby had won.

According to Blair, pills Riggs was slamming down furiously were the equivalent of 2,000 oranges, four pounds of steak and two pounds of liver a day. The liver, apparently, was most critical.

As the match was potentially a five-setter, stamina could be the decider. Liver was fed to certain rats and denied to others. Subsequently, both test groups were tossed into a vat of freezing water. Naturally, they all perished. But those that ate the liver put up the longest fights. 'It's not so cruel,' Riggs stated scientifically. 'There are worse ways to die.' I took this as a kind of prediction. Anyway, Blair stayed close to Bobby to make sure the little rat took his liver.

Salvador Dalí, George Foreman, Jimmy 'The Greek' Snyder and an Arabian sheik along with a Boeing 707 full of his harem hung around the King–Riggs production. Dr Denton Cooley, the Houston heart specialist who gave Bobby a quick physical and got stuck for the fee, wore an 'I've Been Hustled by Bobby Riggs' button. Other buttons read 'Pigs for Riggs' and 'Broads for King'. For the moment, the sports world had gone even loopier than usual. Meanwhile, King kept working and Riggs kept playing. One afternoon, Bud Collins of the *Boston Globe* and the AP's Will Grimsley played Riggs for $5. When the money changed hands, Bobby wanted bigger bills, C notes, substituted for purposes of the photograph. Playfully, he cluttered his side of the court with folding chairs, two and four at a time. If you hit a chair, you won the point. Larry King, not the suspendered talk show host, but the curious husband in Billie Jean's more than curious marriage, challenged Riggs to one of these goofy exercises and lost.

'I was never even that great a junior player,' King shouted from his side of the net.

'I can see that,' said Bobby.

Older brother John Riggs kept nagging, 'Go to bed, Bobby.' But he didn't. Riggs stayed up with the writers and drank and told stories. When the drinking and the storytelling got serious, he said, 'You go ask Kramer or Don Budge if I wasn't the most underrated player of my time. Maybe I was too good a hustler. Maybe I kept some matches too close. Maybe I let some of them . . .' His voice drifted away.

Riggs's moment of grace that week occurred during a joint press conference with Billie Jean when someone asked what he'd do if the 29-year-old woman were his daughter. Everyone waited for a rollicking reply from the scraggly little man peering at Billie Jean through his crooked eyeglasses.

'I'd be very proud of her,' he said.

With highly rare, extremely uncharacteristic prescience, I wrote in my advance column, 'She is an accomplished athlete, perhaps the most accomplished female athlete of the day, and I think she will beat him tonight. It is in the proper order of things that the professional beat the amateur.' But the sight of such a one-sided match was troubling. What Bobby wore in the early going was especially disturbing.

At first, from the Astrodome press box, the spectacle resembled a flea circus. So, following the sedan-chair entrances and the orchestrations of Henry Mancini and the anthem ('I Am Woman') sung by Helen Reddy, a few of us slipped down to courtside and sat like ballboys beside the net. In his haste to relocate, George Cunningham of the *Atlanta Constitution* clumsily dislodged a large slab of the upper deck that would certainly have killed the spectators below whom it narrowly missed.

At courtside, Larry Merchant was collecting room numbers and feverishly whispering up his new football and gambling book, *The National Football Lottery*. (Magically, a copy of it appeared under a sheet of newspaper outside my hotel door the following morning.) In the champagne-soaked bedlam around the court, among Ethel Kennedy, Andy Williams, Merv Griffin and Eva Gabor, a calliope seemed to be playing.

King was quick; Riggs was sluggish. She was gritty in the match's few tight moments; he had absolutely no second serve. Of all things, Bobby seemed to have lost his nerve, 6–4, 6–3, 6–3.

And, for the longest time, he kept his windbreaker on as he played (indoors). It said 'Sugar Daddy' on the back, the brand name of a sucker. Obviously, he was paid to wear it.

In my column the next morning, I concentrated on her triumph ('I wanted to change the game since I was 11 and was kept out of a picture because I didn't have a tennis dress'), but I wondered then, and I wonder now, if Riggs didn't think these things came in threes. Collins and others who know tennis much better than I do believe it was a square deal. So, I'm probably wrong. 'Ain't gonna be no rematch,' King's eyes and tone said much clearer than either Rocky Balboa or Apollo Creed in a clinch. Bobby looked especially stunned at that. 'I have to be the biggest bum of all time now,' he said. Nobody could argue with that.

I finished the column this way: 'He wanted a rematch, but nobody seemed interested or looked like they would be interested ever again. The significance of the entire episode may be simply that there is a great woman athlete, and how many more must there be?'

'Welcome to my world,' Steffi said as we stepped out of the hotel in West Berlin and danced sideways through the paparazzi across the street to an Italian restaurant. Her father, Peter, followed at a trot like a horse who had trouble changing leads.

'Every day,' he said at the table, 'there she was, waiting for me at the door. "Please play with me, Papa." Not four years old.'

Amazed that a three-year-old had the wrist strength for a real tennis grip, he placed her two hands carefully on the racquet and then set her loose on the house. 'We strung the furniture with string for a net,' he said. 'One or two days later, all of the lamps were gone.'

She picked up the string and the story. 'We played for ice cream,' she said, 'ice cream with hot raspberries. There was music, too. It was fun.'

Steffi had yet to win Wimbledon or the US Open, but she hadn't lost a tennis match in seven months. Her arrival at the top of the game was imminent, inevitable. She was 17.

Peter Graf's English was fairly good, but not as good as his daughter's, and it frustrated him to miss even a single word of our conversation. As we rattled on, she laughed comfortably at his discomfort and teased him ragged with partial translations.

It was sweet and obvious that he threw her no chill and that she loved him. Of all the world's little league parents, tennis may produce the most virulent specimens. Andrea Yeager and Tracy Austin were past examples. Mary Pierce and Jennifer Capriati would break new ground. With stress fractures and pelvic injuries, Yeager could match X-rays with most linebackers. In pigtails and pink pinafores, Austin was the spitting image of Patty McCormack in *The Bad Seed*, swearing to her mother that she hadn't set fire to the handyman. As a stage father, Peter Graf was, to my eye anyway, overrated. While he had complete charge of his daughter's finances – and would sit in a German tax jail for a while to prove it – he did not have complete charge of her. 'You can push a good player to become better,' Steffi said straightforwardly, without any apology for the word she was about to apply to herself, 'but it is not possible to push a great player to do anything. When I'm on the court, I don't play for my father. I'm responsible for myself.'

Peter had been a soccer player of local note, given to working excessively hard, to the point of routinely ripping muscles and powdering bones. In this department, Steffi was very much her father's daughter.

She would win more than a hundred tournaments, including seven Wimbledons, five US Opens, six French Opens and four Australian Opens, and cry herself to sleep near the end from back, knee and shoulder pains. She would be No. 1 in the world for 377 weeks, a record.

In Hamburg, a spectator named Guenter Parche, who had lightless eyes, the kind that horrified Boris Becker, would come out of the crowd in the middle of a match to stab Monica Seles in the back with a kitchen knife. Parche regarded Monica as Graf's main competition and he thought of Steffi as 'a dream creation, whose eyes radiate like diamonds, whose hair shines like silk'. Seles received the stitches, but both women were scarred.

As much as Boris would be famous for a blatantly happy smile, Steffi would become known for a somehow sad intensity. He would go on to a career in woman-handling with decidedly mixed results, marry someone other than Mademoiselle Courtin and eventually divorce. Like Peter Graf, Boris would find himself in German tax hell, but he would avoid the Kooler. At Becker's Hall of Fame induction, Ion Tiriac would be the presenter. In his memoirs, Boris would reveal a drinking problem and an addiction to sleeping pills.

Meanwhile, Steffi would replace Brooke Shields in the Andre Agassi corner of the 'friends' box'. Steffi and Andre would wed and have a family. She would be the biggest reason for Andre's remarkable renaissance in his decrepit 30s. And her smile would improve slightly.

They just wanted to be heroes, small and good kind of heroes, even though they knew heroes had very short lives.

At the restaurant in West Berlin, by the time dessert came, Steffi had not said one thing that was even remotely sad. But then she did. 'Someday I might like to own a hotel,' she mused, looking out the window at our hotel across the street, 'try to manage it. I know what's nice about them.' She was 17 and her areas of expertise were forehands and hotels. The dessert was ice cream with hot raspberries.

3

Larry and Oscar

Like a praying mantis trying to get comfortable on a lawn chair, Kareem Abdul-Jabbar stretched out as best he could over a hotel couch in Houston that couldn't come close to containing all of his haunches, hinges and high-tension wires.

'At first,' he said, 'basketball was something I did when the lights were on in the playground, just because I liked it.' He was Lew Alcindor then, a bookish Harlem Catholic who developed a hopping hook shot out of necessity, because most of his straightforward attempts were being blocked.

'I saw a movie, *Go, Man, Go!*, about the Harlem Globetrotters. In one scene, Marques Haynes dribbles past Abe Saperstein in a hotel corridor. After that, I worked at handling the ball. I didn't want to be just a good big man. I wanted to be a good little man, too.'

He had to come to terms with his size, estimated at 7 ft 2 in. 'In school,' he said, 'I was ashamed that my head was so high over the rest of the class. I searched for positive role models so I could be proud of myself. For a long time, I couldn't find any.'

'But you eventually did?' I asked him.

'Yes.'

'Who were they?'

'I'm not sure I want to say.'

'Wilt [Chamberlain]?'

'Are you crazy?'

We laughed together, but Kareem stopped first.

'The Empire State Building,' he said softly. 'The redwood trees.'

Of all the caravans in sports, basketball's were the most intimate. Because of their numbers, baseball and football teams always travelled on chartered planes and customarily filled out the cabins with lawyers, advertising men and other supernumeraries. But a basketball troupe typically consisted of a dozen players, a coach or two, a writer or three, a radio broadcaster who was his own engineer and a combination trainer–travel secretary who taped the ankles and organised the plane tickets.

We waited with everyone else for undependable commercial departures, inevitably the first flight out in the morning, the only defence against a huge fine for blowing a winter game. So the band was up every day around 5 a.m., bleary-eyed vaudevillians playing one-night stands.

On a hotel van to the airport, the topic among the Celtics who weren't still comatose was rock-and-roll music.

'Who's Bruce Springsteen?' Larry Bird wanted to know.

The first one to get his breath back, the *Boston Globe*'s Dan Shaughnessy, answered perfectly. 'Larry, he's the you of rock 'n' roll.'

Bird sighed. 'Where have I been?'

On a basketball court, of course.

With a very good eye and a pretty good mind, Bird grew up in the southern Indiana town of French Lick. He sharpened his eye in endless games of schoolyard 'horse' and wasted his mind in the process. 'Wasted' may be too strong. 'Neglected' is better.

It isn't precisely true that he thought only of basketball, but he thought of everything else only in terms of basketball. He perfunctorily went to class and mechanically did his homework only because he noticed that the kids who skipped class and ditched homework were the same ones who missed the foul shot in the end.

His best friend was that way. In high school, when the other players practised free throws at 6.30 in the morning, his friend slept in. At the regional finals their senior year, the friend missed the front half of three one-and-ones and the team lost in overtime. Nothing was said afterwards. But when their eyes met in the locker room, they both felt a collision of parting. The one going on to college was filled with unbelievable loneliness.

Bird lasted exactly 24 days at Indiana University. In years to come, the common assumption would be that he was intimidated by coach Bobby Knight, an undisciplined disciplinarian given to ordering haircuts while throwing furniture. In fact, nothing about basketball daunted Bird. Everything about Bloomington did.

Just the process of registering for classes was overwhelming. The thought of attending them was petrifying. Suddenly self-conscious about his countrified grammar, he sat mute in the midst of his new society. Actually, what finally put him to rout was the chilling sight of a half-empty closet. His roommate was a preppy little guard named Jim Wisman, who as a sophomore would attain a kind of immortality as the party of the second part in a famous photograph in which Coach Knight is tugging at a player so vehemently that the uniform shirt is straining like a bowstring. Wisman's side of the closet brimmed with herringbone jackets, button-down shirts and madras ties. After waiting for Wisman to fall asleep, Bird silently packed his few pullovers and jeans and hitchhiked back to French Lick, the weary old spa town that, in its day, provided sulphurous cures to Al Capone and FDR. Knight is not the type to chase after any player who runs away, but something about this boy made him wish he could be softer. 'Have you seen him lately, Coach?' someone asked about a year later. 'You ought to see him. He has shot up from 6 ft 6 in. to 6 ft 9 in.' Besides growing, Larry spent the year cutting grass, painting park benches, manning a municipal garbage truck and imagining a life in construction. His father, a wood finisher at the Kimball Piano & Organ Company, killed himself that year with a pistol. His father had gone directly from eighth grade to a life of work. Still awash in basketball offers, Larry decided to try again, at Indiana State in Terre Haute.

As long as he could remember, he had dreamed of glorious victories on the basketball court. But, it's funny, in none of his dreams did he ever make the winning shot. He always made the good passes. So this was the way he played. Without much help, he almost took Indiana State to a national championship. Earvin 'Magic' Johnson and a better supporting cast took Michigan State instead. Accepting the College Player of the Year trophy, Bird showed how reticent and rural he still was by the inappropriately casual clothing he wore to the luncheon and the solitary word he uttered to the assembly. 'How's your finger?' the presenter asked. 'Broke,' he replied.

Crafty Red Auerbach had already claimed him for Boston through a junior-eligible loophole, and the floundering Celtics immediately were themselves again. Alumnus Bob Cousy declared he had never seen such a passer. Old centre Bill Russell said this was a player who would improve everyone else on the court. Away from the court, Bird worked to improve himself. In the middle of a three-year run as the National Basketball Association's Most Valuable Player, he was spotted in the Oakland airport reading Arthur Schlesinger Jr's thick paperback *Robert F. Kennedy and His Times*. Glancing up from page eighty-eight, he moaned, 'This is going to take me three years.'

'Then why are you reading it?' I asked him.

'I dunno, I saw a made-for-TV movie . . .'

This was a lie.

He was reading it because a man who lives in Boston has to know something about the Kennedys.

Basketball couldn't be his whole life, could it? 'Last summer,' he said with a wry laugh, 'I caught myself shooting around one day for five hours. I thought, "What's wrong with me?"'

As Bird strode through the Oakland terminal, the public plumped and patted him in that way they do that takes some getting used to. 'Everyone wants to be a part of something, I understand that now,' he whispered aside. 'In college I didn't. But I've gotten better.'

On the plane, he took the least convenient seat for himself in order to accommodate me, insisting to one teammate after another that I was with the *New York Times Magazine*. Larry seemed unable to hold the concept of *Time* magazine in his head.

Bird and Wayne Gretzky, the reigning Most Valuable Players for the defending world champions, would be together on the cover of *Time*. The proposition was that they were fundamentally the same person: straw-haired country boys, one too fragile for the business, the other too agile for his size. (The day I went to see Gretzky, believe it or not, free concert tickets were being passed around the Edmonton locker room, and Gretzky wanted to know, 'Who's Neil Diamond?' Where had he been?)

Bird and Gretzky saw and played their games from the same vantage point, several moves ahead of the moment, comprehending not only where everything was but also where everything would be. Shown photographs of unremarkable instants on the ice – like the wall decorations in the Oiler offices – Gretzky could place the unpictured performers here and there around the borders and even recall what became of them the next second. Glancing at the basketball photo in the morning paper, Bird's automatic thought, essentially a reflex, was to note what time the photographer had to snap the picture in order to make the deadline.

'I'll be going to Brantford, Ontario, to see Gretzky's little brother,' I told Bird. 'Then I'm off to French Lick to see yours.'

'Do you know Bob Ryan?' he asked.

'Of the *Globe*? Sure.'

'I knew him for six years before I let him go to French Lick.'

'Larry,' I said, 'I'm not applying for a visa. I'm going to French Lick. I'm sure I can show myself that burg in five minutes.'

He laughed, at first silently and then loudly. 'I'll make you a deal. Leave my little brother alone – he's as shy as I used to be – and I'll have my big brother pick you up.'

Done.

As a boy, Bird was not so much aware of the NBA, either at seven or seventeen. He knew everything about every contemporary Indiana high school basketball star, but he never saw Elgin Baylor on television. What little lore he had, he drew from a French Lick dwarf called Shorty, proprietor of Shorty's Pool Hall, who informed Larry and his brothers that their father had been a terrific basketball player and might have gone places had he not left school after the eighth grade and succumbed to a tragic thirst.

'People always ask me, "Who's the best of all time?"' Bird said. 'I have no idea. People probably tend to forget how good players really were. I'm definitely one of the top ones today, but calling anyone the best ever is too harsh a statement. I put myself in the same category with John Havlicek, someone I know worked for everything he got. Who do you say was the best?'

That's an easy question to answer but a hard answer to explain.

Oscar Robertson, of course.

No other basketball player in history had the stamina of Michael Jordan, who was like the best fastball. Hitters swear the good fastballs rise, but the truth is, they just don't fall as precipitously as the others. In the fourth quarter, Jordan probably wasn't moving any quicker than he was in the first; he only seemed to be in relation to the nine other bodies on the court.

Few players were ever as dependable as Jordan at the buzzer, although Jerry West was pretty good. But, to a certain taste – here comes the sacrilege – there have been players just as watchable, even a little more watchable. Early Earl Monroe comes to mind, when he was with Gus Johnson in Baltimore, or Johnson alone when he was against Dave DeBusschere of New York, or George Gervin, or Connie Hawkins, or Baylor, or Julius Erving, obviously.

While graceful certainly, elegant actually, Oscar was not what you would call a watchable player. Maddeningly, he dribbled the ball, like a yo-yo on a string. He didn't just command games, he commandeered them. Sometimes, when he was upset with a teammate, or more often with a referee, he took games over completely. He iron-handedly ran the circus and turned the ball over about once a month.

Bigger and better athletes who would come along, such as Magic Johnson, were capable of much greater wonders. But they were also capable of letting the 24-second clock expire in the process of performing them. On the run, they saw colours, flashes of jerseys. Oscar saw personalities. He saw everything. If the elastic-legged forward Jumpin' Johnny Green was one step beyond his modest shooting range, Johnny might as well have been standing in the parking lot. Oscar had a clock in his head, a metronome. He knew everybody's foul situation. Hell, he knew everybody's marital situation. He made calculations upon calculations. You could see him doing it.

To Robertson, basketball was simple geometry. If you gave him a 20-footer, he wanted an 18-footer. If you gave him an 18-footer, he wanted a 16-footer. He was constantly closing in on the basket. Oscar stood only 6 ft 4 in. or so but he was stronger up top than the men guarding him, like West. When Oscar finally shot, he floated aloft in a reverse C, balancing the ball in one hand over his head, a little behind his head, as unhurriedly as Ernie Els setting a golf club.

Robertson waited for the foul, and waited, and waited, and if he made the basket and didn't get a free throw on top of it, he recoiled down the court angrily to pick up the defence, a chest-to-chest defence that was less frenzied but more effective than today's hand-checking and shot-blocking, not to mention clubbing and mauling. Nobody ever went coast-to-coast for a lay-up in those days.

Until almost the very end, Oscar's entire career was largely a frustration. Pete Newell, the stately University of California coach, confounded him twice in the Final Four of the NCAAs. Newell's system was rudimentary: make sure that whenever Oscar gave up the ball, he didn't get it back. Before the semi-final game of 1959, Bob Dalton, an average but mischievous Cal guard, proffered his hand to Oscar and said, 'My name's Dalton. What's yours?'

Newell also coached the US Olympic team in 1960, a roster of saints that included Oscar, West, Jerry Lucas, Walt Bellamy, Terry Dischinger and Adrian 'Odie' Smith. (Havlicek, a sophomore, was one of the final cuts.) In Rome, out of a compassion that would seem quaint come 'Dream Team' days, Newell played Robertson at forward instead of guard because he thought putting Oscar in charge of the ball against Japan amounted to Ugly Americanism. As it was, their closest games were around 40 points.

In that NBA era of territorial drafts, Robertson of the University of Cincinnati joined Lucas of Ohio State, Smith of

Kentucky and Wayne Embry of Miami University (in Oxford, Ohio) on a worthy Cincinnati Royals team that could win 55 of 81 games during the regular season but could never get past that impenetrable pick set by Boston's Bill Russell, who over 13 years in varied company won 11 world championships.

Moving to Milwaukee for the last chapter, by this time smuggling a small basketball in his stomach, Robertson spoon-fed young Kareem Abdul-Jabbar his first of six NBA titles ('No nonsense, no frills,' Jabbar told me. 'Playing with Oscar was a privilege'); and, just briefly, Robertson smiled. That's when I knew him.

The custom of the day was to put the visiting writer, usually just one writer, at the end of the courtside press table right next to the visiting coach. For a time, I sat beside New Yorker Jack McMahon as he tried to get Elvin Hayes to play nicely with Rick Adelman, Jim Barnett, John Block, Stu Lantz and the rest of the San Diego Rockets. Turning to me once after a timeout, McMahon enquired, 'Isn't this grotesque?'

'"I-s-n-'t t-h-i-s g-r-o-t-e-s-q-u-e?" M-c-M-a-h-o-n s-a-i-d,' I typed into my running story.

'How's it going?' I greeted Jack at the San Diego Sports Arena the following morning.

'*The* dumbest question I've ever been asked,' he said.

McMahon was fired that afternoon, replaced by Wilt Chamberlain's old sparring partner, Alex Hannum. I asked McMahon if he had any regrets. He said he had only one regret in a life of basketball. Referring to a previous station with the Royals, he said, 'I once begged Oscar to play.'

At home games, I worked in the middle of the table, next to the clock operator, where the reporting players waiting for a horn sat like Camp Fire girls on the floor. Bucks coach Larry Costello habitually gave Oscar a little blow with five or six minutes to go and then reinserted him for the last couple of minutes to win the close games. Almost unfailingly, he did win them. Except, one night in San Diego, as Robertson was waiting to re-enter, his head fell back against my typewriter, stopping the carriage in mid-sentence. I was on a tight deadline.

Oscar uniformly disdained all writers but felt a particular enmity for the *Cincinnati Enquirer*'s Barry McDermott, who had sided with Royals coach Bob Cousy in the great Cousy–Robertson war. It was easy for a writer to fall in love with Cousy, a sentimental character equally liable to cry in your arms or wave a fist in your face. Most seductive of all, he was relentlessly frank and thoroughly honest.

The moribund Royals had few enough occasions to celebrate. Yet, one night, after a rousing home victory over Chamberlain's Lakers, Cousy opened his post-game comments with 'Well, Wilt barely showed up tonight.'

Of course it was true. But did he have to say it? Later, I asked him why he insisted on throwing cold water at his own players.

'Because I've made my fucking money,' he said. 'I'm just not going to lie anymore.'

Robertson was still with the Royals when, in a transparent attempt to sell tickets, Cousy put a uniform back on and made an awful fool of himself. Now he was poaching on Oscar's territory. Possibly, Bob was jealous of Robertson. The next generation always comes in for more money. Also, although Cousy had been a pioneer in the players' union, it was Oscar who was the association's president when the players filed the anti-trust action that won them their free agency. Robertson's name is on the landmark suit.

From Cousy's side, though, it should also be said that Oscar was only a perfect player. He was not a perfect delight.

As McDermott and others observed, a groin wrap that intermittently appeared on Robertson's thigh seemed to be a convenient dressing for hurt feelings. (This is what McMahon was talking about, 'begging' Oscar to play.) Many of Barry's dispatches throbbed more than Oscar's thigh, with sarcasm. They tended to begin this way: Oscar Robertson (comma) who has played ten years in the NBA without a floor burn (comma) . . . Until, finally, the unthinkable was thinkable in Cincinnati, and The Big O was traded to Milwaukee.

Mindlessly, when the carriage of my Olivetti snagged against the back of Robertson's haircut, I did something unusually stupid, even for me. Instead of just saying, 'Move, Oscar,' I leaned forward and whispered in Robertson's ear, 'Hey, O, what do you hear from Barry McDermott?' He went off like a Roman candle.

Papers flew. Typewriters bounced. The table all but went over.

Hypocritically, I looked left and right like everyone else who was wondering what could have turned Robertson into Rumpelstiltskin. When the storm blew over, Oscar went into the game, missed every shot he took, and, for the first time since their Astrodome summit in college, Hayes beat Abdul-Jabbar. Elvin burst into tears. In his memoirs, he dedicated a whole section to this great breakthrough. I never had the heart to tell him.

After handing off a first-edition lead to the Western Union lady, I went to the Bucks locker room, where a large, gentle forward named Bob Boozer was standing sentry in uniform. 'You do not want to come in here,' he said.

'I have to see Oscar.'

'No, no, no. You don't. You don't. Believe me, you don't.'

'I do.'

'Then do *not* leave my side,' Boozer said.

In the locker room, the Milwaukee players were hurriedly changing clothes, motivated to speed by the sound of Robertson in the lavatory beating up a urinal. Boozer and I entered gingerly. Oscar screamed for a little while and I shut up. He spoke quietly for a much longer while and I listened. Boozer slipped away and I started to understand.

Oscar was born in Charlotte, Tennessee, a small town south of Clarksville. He was the son of a divorced sanitation worker who moved his children to the dusty side of Indianapolis when Oscar was four. Indiana was the cradle of two American institutions: basketball, particularly high school basketball, and Nathan Bedford Forrest's Ku Klux Klan.

Robertson went to segregated Crispus Attucks High School, named for a black revolutionary, the first man shot dead in a skirmish that led to the Boston Tea Party. 'It was a Klan school,' Oscar said, sitting on the bathroom floor with his head against the wall. 'It was where the Klan put the blacks to keep them away from the whites.' I sat down at the opposite wall. The first-edition story I had sent the paper would have to stand up all night. I wouldn't have time to sub it.

As a sophomore, Robertson learned the game. As a junior and senior, he taught it. The Tigers won 62 of 63 games Oscar's last two years and a pair of state championships. On the eve of the first title, the mayor of Indianapolis came to Crispus Attucks and the principal summoned a schoolwide assembly.

Speaking to me in a low voice, Oscar said, 'We were told that, if we won, there was to be no celebration. There would be no parade through the middle of the city, as there always was for the white teams. They didn't want to hear a single horn honk. They didn't want to hear a single cheer. Just clear out of Monument Circle and don't smash any lampposts on your way. They didn't want any trouble.'

When the Tigers did win, they quietly loaded their family cars and streamed to a remote park, into the woods, really, escorted by the Indianapolis police, for a pep rally and a laugh and a song. Oscar didn't laugh and he didn't sing.

The gymnasium at Crispus Attucks was below substandard.

Even on the most numbing winter days, the Tigers often found it convenient to practise outdoors. As they became more and more renowned, they played more and more of their home games in Butler Fieldhouse, the cavernous gym featured in the Gene Hackman movie *Hoosiers*. The film is based on Indiana's fabled state basketball tournament and the unlikely triumph of a minuscule school, Milan, renamed 'Hickory' by the screenwriters.

Milan's storied season occurred in Oscar's sophomore year, 1953–54. Crispus Attucks lost to Milan early in the tournament, 65–52 (Oscar's only loss in 28 tournament games; he scored 22 points). In the movie, the first blacks in the picture are brought in at the very end to lose the final game and pound the floor with their fists. Imagine Robertson, sitting in the dark of a theatre, watching his old coach, Ray Crowe, portraying himself, or the Muncie Central coach, or somebody.

Crowe's brother, George, was Indiana's first 'Mr Basketball' in 1939 and was later a first baseman for the Cincinnati Reds. Consider a black high school basketball player good enough to be called 'Mister' in 1939. D.C. Stevenson, the KKK descendant of Nathan Bedford Forrest, kept the blacks of Indianapolis, Evansville and Gary out of the state tournament before 1943. When he wasn't hand-picking Indiana political officials all the way up to the governor, Stevenson was dreaming of buying Valparaiso University and turning it into the Klan equivalent of the nearby Catholic college, Notre Dame. All of that fell through when Stevenson was convicted of sexually assaulting and killing a secretary on a train to Chicago.

When Oscar held the title of Mr Basketball, he was a figure of local awe. Tom Van Arsdale, who would later share the same distinction with his twin brother, Dick, and in fact would end up playing alongside Oscar in the NBA, met Robertson for the first time at a high school track meet.

'I was still in grade school,' Van Arsdale later told me. 'Oscar was wearing a letter jacket, eating a hot dog. I asked him for his autograph. I'll never forget it. He put the hot dog in his jacket pocket, mustard and all, and signed the wrapper. You can't imagine how big he was to me.'

Like Indiana, neighbouring Kentucky also had a Mr Basketball – white, of course – a hotshot from Wayland, Kentucky, with the fabulous name King Kelly Coleman. That year, the annual Indiana–Kentucky High School All-Star Series amounted to a match race between King Kelly and Robertson.

The Indiana stars won the first game in Indianapolis, 92–78. King Kelly scored 17 points. Oscar had 34.

Come the rematch in Louisville, all of the pre-game talk was of vengeance and redemption. Coleman promised to take personal charge of Robertson, to battle him head-to-head, both offence and defence, for every minute of the game.

And he did.

This time, King Kelly scored four points in a 102–79 Indiana victory. Oscar had 41.

Yet neither the University of Kentucky nor Indiana University was at all interested in recruiting Robertson. Kentucky coach Adolph Rupp's position was self-evident. Once, when the Baron grew excited over a high school player's statistics before he realised the player's complexion, he drawled, 'You'd think they'd put an *asterisk* after their names.'

Coach Branch McCracken of IU was an avuncular bear from a small southern Indiana town who came to coexist with a string of black tokens forced on him by the university one at a time. But there was no vacancy when Oscar and Coach Crowe came to see McCracken with their hats in their hands.

'I'd have done anything,' Robertson told me through gritted teeth. 'I'd have died to go to IU.'

He and McCracken had a curious, jumbled conversation, something about Oscar not being the type to 'extort' under-the-table money from a school. 'I didn't know what the hell he was talking about,' Oscar said, and Robertson never heard from McCracken again.

At the University of Cincinnati, Oscar experienced the usual slights of the day, especially when the team travelled in the South. He stayed at black colleges when the hotels wouldn't take him. He found the requisite number of black cats in his locker. Closer to home, there were cafés and movie houses in the shadow of his own campus that wouldn't accommodate him.

These things happened everywhere, to everyone of colour.

The difference between Oscar and the other black athletes of the era was that he could never let any of it go. He still can't. He was so bitter that it broke his teammates' hearts. There's a certain kind of bitterness that just makes you want to cry.

Oscar found a perfect thing to do and a perfect place to do it, but the only way he could do it was with defiance.

He showed them. He showed them. He showed them.

Robertson never looked back to see himself as a unifying point, a contradictor of stereotypes, a changer of attitudes, a unanimously proclaimed Indianan, a man whose influence on the state was more profound than that of Nathan Bedford Forrest and D.C. Stevenson times a thousand, a black basketball player who didn't come dribbling out of the womb, who is remembered especially for his brain.

And who had a heart.

In 1997, when Robertson gave his 33-year-old daughter a kidney, he bristled at the testimonials. 'Who wouldn't do that for a daughter?' he asked with his old scowl. What were they getting at, complimenting him this way? What was behind it? What did they mean? When the University of Cincinnati erected a statue to him, he shook and bawled at the unveiling, not with release and redemption but with black cats and rage.

'He must have been something,' Bird said quietly, after a long moment.

It took me another moment to answer him.

'I guess I wouldn't trade Jordan for him, or Magic, or you,' I said. 'But he was something, all right. He *had* something. He was even better than the three of you at something.'

'Yeah,' Bird said. 'Basketball.'

Larry's older brother, Mark, was waiting for me in French Lick. He was a shorter, fleshier version, but unmistakable, right down to the buttermilk moustache.

'Are you the guy from the *New York Times Magazine?*' he asked when I put out my hand.

'Yep.'

We toured the town, including Larry Bird Boulevard, marked by a circular standard, larger than a Gulf sign, and ended up at the Springs Valley High School gymnasium, where a Bird mural stared down from over an exit sign like a chapel Madonna.

Larry ultimately made it his business to find out who Bruce Springsteen was. He had confused him, it turned out, with Rick Springfield. 'I'm still not into loud music,' Bird told me a couple of hours before a game in New York, as we bounced a ball back and forth at Madison Square Garden, 'but you should see how hard that Springsteen works for four hours. By the time it's about through, you're sick of him, but he still wants to go more. Whew, it wore me out. He's great.'

Leave it to Bird to admire a man for his perspiration.

For ten professional years, Larry played beautifully, trying to broaden himself as he went. For two or three more, he played haltingly, on deteriorating bones. At the end, he played in the Olympics, scoring no points in his final professional game. He made the good passes.

When he stepped up to a podium in Boston to say goodbye, he brought more than one word this time. He came with humour, touch, depth, style, grace and the thing he always had: honesty. There was a life for him to turn to, a wife and a new baby. A hundred years ago, he and a cheerleader had had a daughter and parted. A thousand years ago.

In his farewell address, he timed the jokes to avoid the tears, and the effect was surprisingly joyful. The message was unspoken but understood. The impulse was to cheer.

He was more than just a basketball player, after all.

A Nets bag was found in the wreckage of the plane.

It turned out to belong to an ex-Net, Wendell Ladner, a sweet, dim, handsome man from Necaise Crossing, Mississippi, who went to his death believing the Washington Monument was the *Washington Post*. Gazing out the window on a previous flight, Wendell had asked the wrong person, a sportswriter, 'What is that?'

To get to the funeral in Necaise Crossing, you had to fly to Biloxi and drive quite a ways through fields of scrawny cows, each one balancing a white bird on her back, and legions of tin Nehi soft drink signs, and scores of rickety logging shacks. And, when you finally got as deep as you could go into the woods, Julius Erving was the only teammate waiting.

'That's a memory right there,' said Dr J., sitting in one of his last locker rooms, collecting memories. 'Old Wendell Ladner.'

Erving told me, 'I'm savouring a lot of old moves and a lot of old players because they should be savoured, don't you think? I've borrowed from every player I've ever seen, from the little guard with the two-handed set shot to the big centre with the slam dunk to the forward defending the passing lanes like a free safety in football.'

In the nearly empty room, Julius was icing his knees, which by this time practically bent both ways. 'I'll tell you something,' he added with a spark of surprise. 'The ending has the same innocence attached to it that the beginning had. I feel light and free. I feel relieved.'

4

Plus Fours

This is the story of a retired milkman named Emil Kijek, who wound up his life in the arms of a friend in the middle of a fairway on a Thursday afternoon. The setting is south-east Massachusetts, on the rim of Narragansett Bay, where stories this small are usually thrown back. Lizzie Borden hailed from Fall River, right next door; Ishmael and Ahab sailed from New Bedford, just down the road.

Ron Collett, Morris Dumont, Jack Alexander and Kijek — whom everyone but Alexander called 'Ky' — were teamed up that Thursday in a senior tournament at the Sun Valley Golf Club. 'Ky had a spirit about him,' said Dumont, a retired piano tuner. 'He was the type who enjoyed the day better than the golf, who took the good shots and bad shots as they came, always hoping the next one would be perfect.'

Ky had been a Seabee during the Second World War, a builder; also, a boxer. He was an only son who had an only daughter, Sandra, whose childhood memories were of spontaneous picnics and Sunday motor rides.

As a golfer, Kijek was a good, straight hitter, even at the age of 79, an 11- or 12-handicapper who held to that number, as his distance waned, with increasingly better putting. This phenomenon is unheard of in the pros but well known in places like Sun Valley.

'You're saving us, Old Man,' Alexander said after Ky followed a 20-footer at the first hole with another handy putt at the fourth.

The sixth hole at Sun Valley is a 155-yard par three. Kijek took a three-wood. 'He hit that thing so beautifully,' Dumont would say later. 'It had this amazing trajectory.'

'Emil, I can't see the ball,' Alexander murmured after a moment. 'I think it went in the hole.'

'Naw,' Kijek said. In his entire life, he'd never had a hole in one.

'Old Man!' Alexander shouted as they reached the green. 'Come get your ball out of the cup!'

Ky was thrilled beyond measure, but there was no jumping up and down. He was a humble man.

After driving nicely at the seventh, he wavered more than a moment over his second shot.

'Emil,' Alexander said gently, 'let somebody else hit first.'

'No, no, I'm OK, Jack,' he said.

In the next instant, Kijek started to fall, and Alexander caught him. They settled softly in the grass. As the others ran for help, Jack said, 'Emil, squeeze my hand. Don't stop until I tell you to.' But Ky looked up at his best friend, smiled and let go.

Some days afterward, in the clubhouse, which was mostly a bar, I had a beer with the proprietor, John Pellegrino. He said people kept asking him about Emil Kijek. 'Who was he?' they wanted to know.

He was a man who enjoyed the day better than the golf, who took the good shots and bad shots as they came, always hoping the next one would be perfect.

And it was.

ONE

A few of Payne Stewart's obituaries included the well-meaning twaddle that Stewart's trademark plus fours represented a nod to antiquity. But, the truth was, he wore 'knickers' for the same reason Jerry Pate used to swan dive into water hazards, to try to distinguish himself from a multitude of towheads. The loud colours *were* a kind of tribute to the past, mimicking, as they did, the paisley prints and checkered patterns of his father, Bill, a travelling salesman. Bill Stewart was a showy man who loved to take his wife, Bee, to the dance clubs on Saturday nights. Little Payne learned the basics of the ballroom standing on his dad's toes in the living room. In the son's case, the clothes didn't make the man; they just made him known. A cherished by-product of Payne's ensembles was that, when he threw off his disguise, he almost completely disappeared. One time, his three pro-am partners all showed up in costume, only to find Stewart standing there in khaki trousers and a ball cap. The amateurs were crestfallen.

During the years that Stewart and Tom Kite shared Texas coach Chuck Cook, they often played practice rounds together. If Stewart and Kite weren't the most dissimilar men on the PGA Tour, they were in the hunt. Admittedly, too much could be made of Kite's mechanics and Stewart's aesthetics. Tom also had a melody. Payne also worked hard. But, sharing their company for a week at Pebble Beach, I couldn't let go of the notion that, if the two were somehow spliced into one, he would have been the greatest golfer who ever lived. (Well, maybe the second-greatest.)

Cook was caddieing for me in the AT&T as part of a story, so I was sort of crashing the party. Kite was more than agreeable. It meant he could see Cook without paying Chuck's way. Stewart was less comfortable. His propensity for putting a gold-tipped boot in his mouth was high enough without letting the biographers inside the ropes.

At closest range, Stewart's shots sounded crisper than Kite's, or anyone's. In Payne's hands, via that long, loose swing, the irons were tuning forks playing a crystal song of silver on glass. He could fall out of the car and hit a golf ball, and then hit another one, and another, pulling on his spikes as he went.

Kite was the kind who had to understand the molecular structure of things, but Cook knew not to overload Stewart's computer with technicalities. If a certain course made a lower ball-flight desirable, Kite would consult Galileo and Copernicus. Meanwhile, Cook might remark offhandedly to Stewart, 'Hey, Payne, I don't remember the ball being that far forward in your stance.' Grunting, Stewart would bump the ball back slightly and all would be well. A week later, when the higher trajectory came back into fashion, Cook would muse, with a yawn, 'Hmm, I wonder if we overcompensated last week.' Payne nudged the ball forward and carried on.

'They're going too straight,' Stewart once complained on a practice tee. He was hitting tracers into the clouds.

'Straight's OK,' Cook said from behind. 'I like straight. Let's settle for straight.'

'Nooo,' Stewart said, 'I want to see it move one way or the other.' This may sound goofy but, you know, Jack Nicklaus initially became a left-to-right player just because he loved the sight of the ball tumbling that way out of the Midwestern sky.

Which is not to say Stewart wasn't goofy. He was major-league goofy. It is hardly surprising that his final appearance on television was to apologise for a toothy rendition of a Chinaman in response to the observation of English broadcaster Peter Alliss that Americans are so different from Europeans that they might as well be Chinese. 'I didn't mean to make fun of anybody,' Stewart said sincerely.

He was a 'ragger' in the rollicking and heartbreaking sense of the baseball players in *Bang the Drum Slowly*. Sometimes it seemed the cost of knowing him was to take it and dish it out. But he wasn't cruel. It could fairly be stated that, in his time, Stewart at least peeked into a couple of life's darker corners, but with mischief more than malice.

When Yankee catcher Thurman Munson died in a private plane accident in 1979, a memorial was made of his locker and a lot of dishonest 'heart of gold' stuff was said and written. Under Munson's gruff exterior was a gruffer interior. He was a nice catcher, a tremendous clutch hitter and a bitterly unhappy person. Considering the gauzy way Stewart went out, on a Flying Dutchman over South Dakota, his testimonials were, on balance, balanced. After the plane crash, so many of those close to Stewart spoke of a change in him over the previous couple of years that it had to be true.

'He treated me great the whole time I knew him,' Cook told me, 'but he didn't treat everybody that way. In 1989, he was ungracious in victory at the PGA Championship and ungracious in defeat at the Tour Championship – he wouldn't shake Kite's hand. Payne was petulant a lot of the time. I'll tell you, he wasn't really all that well liked by the other players. But, a couple of years ago, he had an attitude change. He started reaching out to people.' The baseball pitcher Orel Hershiser was Stewart's amateur partner at the AT&T. Some said Hershiser was the one who reached out spiritually for Payne. Others said it was the children, Chelsea and Aaron. When ten-year-old Aaron caught a Pop Warner touchdown pass five days after his father died, sort of putting a period on that eerie week, you wondered, where do children, where do people, get such resilience?

But then you remembered that small blonde woman in the Orlando church and thought of her watching the runaway plane on CNN's *Breaking News*, hitting the redial button over and over and intermittently getting a cheery message from her husband between the ringing and ringing of a cell phone in a frozen cabin. As Nicklaus says, golfers only aim for perfection, never achieve it. But golf came fairly close that week. Starting with PGA Commissioner Tim Finchem's decision to play, and pause, and play again, everything that was said and done was right. Paul Azinger gave two eulogies: a happy one (rolling up his pants to the knee) and a sad one, and they were both perfect. Tracey Stewart was magnificent.

At the service, there may have been one preacher too many. And the piper coming out of the fogbank at the first tee recalled the Scots' definition of a gentleman: someone who knows how to play the bagpipes – and doesn't. But those were awfully small warts.

Leaving the church through an honour guard of players, like a military bride at her wedding, Tracey paused to hug fellow Australian Greg Norman especially. Famously, Payne and Greg were not close friends. But it was all right now. Stewart's longtime caddie, Mike Hicks, 'Hicksey', was in the congregation. After their last bogey in the 1999 US Open at Pinehurst, Hicks told Payne, 'Just hang tough, you know how these things go.' He should know. They could have won four of them in the '90s.

'Payne turned to me,' Hicks recalled, 'with this look of unbelievable peace. He didn't have it last year. I say the change was more this year. I don't know how religious you are, but I don't think he was ready to witness last year. He was ready to witness now.'

The first of the three improbable putts that won Payne the Open was, to Hicks's eye, the impossible one. 'Impossible to read, uphill, downhill, breaking two ways, come on. But then I thought, "He's better at the impossible." When he made it, I knew.'

Stewart did not read books. Even at the height of its football prowess, Southern Methodist University probably never produced a worse speller. Attempting to read anything out loud, Stewart brought to mind a panicked third-grader standing up before the entire class. Quite late in the game, he was diagnosed with attention deficit disorder and had a taste of Ritalin. He preferred the taste of tobacco. Stewart was capable of dipping snuff, puffing a cigar and chewing Nicorette gum all at the same time.

The ADD showed up in his golf, especially. The simplest

shots were his weakness; they couldn't hold his interest. Eleven victories on the PGA Tour make a meagre total for a Payne Stewart. The three majors he won, and the many others he nearly won, are more like it.

'For some reason,' Hicks said, 'he could get to a level of focus at the US Open that he could never attain any other week, as much as he tried. I was really looking forward to Pebble Beach.'

When Hicksey finally got there the following June, he was the only amateur lined up with 20 pros to fire a 21-driver salute into the Pacific Ocean. The year that Payne, Kite, Cook and I were together at Pebble, I tried everything to pry a smile out of Stewart. 'When you touch your cap to acknowledge the cheers,' I asked him, 'is it two fingers or three?'

'Two fingers,' he said grimly.

'When you're striding down the fairway with your glove hanging out your back pocket . . .'

'Four fingers,' he said. 'Don't embarrass us.'

At one point, the talk turned to psychology, and the players began comparing notes. Kite was a Bob Rotella man. While Stewart had consulted Rotella in early days, Dick Coop was his regular shrink.

'Callahan's a Rotella guy,' Cook said mischievously. For the story, I had seen Rotella exactly once.

'Really?' Kite said.

'Oh, yeah,' I said. 'I've been seeing Rotella twice a week for four years.'

'*Really?*'

'Sure. We go down to his basement in Charlottesville and I putt at this little hole he has in the carpet.'

'I've putted at that hole!' Kite said.

Now Stewart was interested.

'What advice did he give you for the tournament?' Kite asked.

'Two things,' I said. 'He told me to concentrate on all the good he had done Tom Kite and try to put out of my mind what he did to Payne Stewart.'

Stewart stopped in his tracks. He looked over at me. And, finally, he smiled.

TWO

It was as if God said to Nicklaus, 'You will have skills like no other', then whispered to Palmer, 'but they will love you more'.

Through many seasons of frosts and thaws, at times golf's most complicated relationship included a measure of real warmth and authentic affection. But it never strayed very far from the principle on which it was founded: mutual jealousy. Arnie envied Jack's ability; Jack envied Arnie's lovability. Grace came easily to Palmer; golf came easily to Nicklaus.

Arnold Palmer was the square-backed Pennsylvanian who hoisted a country club game onto his sturdy shoulders, carried it to the people and made it a sport. From the beginning, he looked like an athlete: a prizefighter, a middleweight. In the beginning, Nicklaus looked like a sportswriter, an unmade bed. Palmer was delivered along with the first television sets. Even more winning than his compulsion to go for broke was his inclination not to go alone. He took everyone with him he could carry, and for a while there he was carrying the entire culture. People who didn't follow golf followed him. Second-timers in Palmer's gallery imagined he recognised them and had missed them and wondered where the hell they had been. Although securely married, Palmer would cast his eyes about for feminine inspiration, leaning on his club in a comfortable slouch. He was both a ladies' man and a man's man. He was one of those lucky blokes who get it right merely by being themselves. And the simplest fact of the US Open at Oakmont in 1962 (Palmer country, near Pittsburgh) wasn't really that nobody wanted him beaten by young Nicklaus. It was that nobody wanted him beaten at all.

'Miss it, Fat Guts,' the gallery hissed. Nicklaus, of course, didn't hear. Jack was the overfed Ohioan with the well-schooled swing, ten years younger. Longer than a Midwestern winter, he had a look of eagles and albatrosses. He was ruthlessly thought out, shrewdly calculated, practically calibrated. On the golf course, in talent and in other ways, he was alone.

Now and then during a round, it would occur to Nicklaus that there were actually other people on the property, and where had they all come from? Occasionally he would attempt to acknowledge them with a horribly synthetic wink that always put me in mind of a love letter marked 'Occupant'. Nicklaus wasn't the first person to discover that nobody loves a fat man, but he made characteristic use of the information. He slimmed himself into a model for clothes and a mould for golfers.

At the height of his powers, I drew him for a partner in a pro-am at King's Island in Ohio. Of course, the fix was in. He told me so, but asked me not to let on to the organisers. 'When you wrote that this was a fairly pretty golf course for a blind date,' he said, 'they thought they better try to warm you up.' With Desmond Muirhead, Nicklaus had codesigned the pleasant but homely layout.

'I really don't think we won anything,' I said to Jack, as he checked and rechecked our scorecard afterward.

'I know,' he said. 'I'm just hoping we didn't finish last.'

'You only hit one guy,' shrugged Jack's fright-wigged caddie, Angelo Argea, attempting to console me. (I had hit a guy at ten; hard, too.)

'I don't know, I played better when Creamy Carolan was caddieing,' I said, mentioning Palmer's regular bagman.

'Fuck Creamy Carolan,' Angelo said.

'And . . . no, I'm not going to say it,' Jack laughed.

He and Palmer first brushed at Toledo in 1954, when Arnold was the 23-year-old amateur champion and Nicklaus a 13-year-old dreamer. It was raining steadily and Palmer was the only one on the range, slamming low iron shots under the storm. Naturally, Arnold had no idea who was studying him from the hillside. But then Jack didn't know whom he was studying.

'I sat there and watched this guy practise. He was hitting knock-down 9-irons, just drilling them as low and as hard as he could. I watched him for about an hour in the rain.'

Later, when he realised who it was, Nicklaus said, 'Oh, *that's* Arnold Palmer.' From then on, he followed Arnie from afar, just like everyone else in golf, forever asking, 'What did Palmer do today?'

Before long, a meeting was arranged between the man and the boy, and the man shot 62, and Palmer had tried to shoot 62, to impress the boy. 'I certainly was impressed by him,' Arnold said.

In 1960, when Palmer truly became Palmer, charging to his only US Open championship at Denver's Cherry Hills, the 20-year-old amateur Nicklaus finished second. 'That boy I played with today should have won,' Ben Hogan said. 'If I could have done his thinking for him, he'd have won by ten shots.'

'If I could have putted for Mr Hogan,' Nicklaus said, 'he would have won by ten.' Two years later, Nicklaus and Palmer changed places at Oakmont, forever really. In between those two events, they were, for just a moment, partners. 'In 1961, Arnie came up to me in the locker room at Firestone,' Nicklaus reminisced.

'I want to hear this,' interrupted Palmer, who was sitting beside him now.

'He knew I was thinking of turning pro,' Jack continued, 'and offered to help me in any way he could. Mark

McCormack [Palmer's longtime friend and superagent] came to see me. The prospect of being in the same stable with Arnie was very appealing.'

There was side money to be made in exhibitions and such. In pursuit of it, they won 17 team championships together, flying together, eating together, making a pile of mischief, logging their share of laughter.

'I can think of the ginger ale battles we had in hotel rooms,' Palmer said effervescently.

'I remember one night,' Nicklaus said, 'when we got to kicking each other's shins under the table. I don't know why. I kicked him. He kicked me. Neither would give. We ended up with the biggest damned bruises. We used to do the stupidest stuff.'

Captain Palmer, golf's Wiley Post, loved to bank his private aeroplane and terrorise his groggy passengers, whose numbers swelled by one when McCormack enlisted the peripatetic South African Gary Player and packaged them as golf's 'Big Three'.

'Do you remember that time,' Nicklaus asked Palmer, 'when we were flying out of Seagraves, Texas, and I had to hold on to keep off the ceiling? We were all over the sky.'

Palmer laughed and said, 'I had Player crouching down under the seat, I remember that.'

'I shouldn't laugh,' Nicklaus said. 'But it wasn't always hard-nosed stuff, was it? We had some fun.'

'Laddie is probably on an aeroplane right this minute,' Palmer said, referring to Player. 'The way he tells it, he's always on a plane. By his calculations, he has spent over three years of his life in the air.'

Player is a man of many charming exaggerations, but this is not one of them. Before and after jets, he *has* logged over three years in the sky. It takes some time to believe the little man in black. But that's all right. We have some time.

I visited him once at his ranch in Lanseria, just a half hour north of Johannesburg. Although I had rented a car, Player is a courtly chap and insisted on sending his driver to fetch me. The driver was a young black man named David. Appropriately enough, he was driving a Volkswagen Golf. At the sign for Blair Atholl, Player's spread, David stopped the car for a moment before pulling in. 'Sometimes when you come to a place like this one,' he told me, 'it's like you mustn't go away again.'

We wound our way through a patch of woods to the entrance, where a Joseph Conrad character popped out of a sentry's box and piped me aboard by name. Rolling into the sunlight, we could see horses in training, thoroughbreds, including a high-priced relative of Northern Dancer. Music was in the air, coming from a schoolhouse.

Four hundred black children attend classes every day at Player's home, kindergarten through seventh grade. He started the school with the few children of his workers, and the enrolment grew. The singing of the children filled the property. It lingered with the squeak of gumboot dancing and the smoke of learning.

'Listen,' said Player, who came out of the main house wearing a tan safari suit and a dark brown sombrero. 'Listen to them sing. Some of them barefoot but all of them in a tie and jacket. Isn't it beautiful? Isn't education the light? The children will lead, as usual.'

When the music stopped, Player sang on: 'Open spaces, fresh air, wild animals, beautiful beaches, extraordinary people' – he cannot love his country fast enough. 'Look at this, it's like this every day.'

He was born in 1935, six years after Palmer, five years before Nicklaus. His mother, Muriel, from whom Player inherited his small features, died when Gary was eight. 'She never saw me hit a golf ball,' he said with a sadness that can still call him to the edge of childhood. Unlike a lot of tough guys, Player is utterly unafraid of sentiment.

Maybe you never thought of him as a tough guy, standing just 5 ft 7 in. tall, but Tom Weiskopf and Bruce Crampton have, never mind why. The exaggerated gentlemanliness with which Player coats the pig iron has often been taken for sanctimony. It ought to be thought of as touching.

His father, Harry – 'Whiskey' to his co-workers – was a flushed-face gold miner with corrugated hands but a sweet disposition. With walls and people collapsing all around him, Whiskey Player dug out a meagre living. 'Never in his life,' Gary said, 'did he make $200 a month. We lived in a crummy little house. One day, in 1952, Dad rolled up with a set of Turfrider Wilson clubs. "I had a bit of money," he told me. Years later, I learned from the bank manager that he had taken an overdraft to buy me those clubs.'

At one early tournament, no one could understand why the grim lad in the oversize sweater didn't remove his heavy wool as the chilly morning gave way to a sweltering afternoon. The reason was that, under somebody else's sweater, he was wearing somebody else's trousers, and the beltline washed up practically to his armpits.

It was Harry who wrote the letter to Clifford Roberts at Augusta National that resulted in Player's original invitations to the Masters. Gary was the first foreign player to win the Masters, and to win it, and to win it. Seve Ballesteros and all of the rest are indebted to him.

Like only Gene Sarazen and Hogan before him, and only Nicklaus and Tiger Woods after him, Player won his profession's four great prizes: the Masters, the US Open, the British Open and the PGA Championship (the last forever eluding Palmer). But Gary may be even prouder of being counted in the Big Three. 'Where Arnold changed the game,' he said, 'was the way he looked at people. It made them look at golf.'

Once, on the Senior Tour, Player was lingering by a green in a Maryland suburb of Washington when Palmer, playing in the group just behind, made a hole in one. (The next day, by the way, Arnold aced the same hole again; the third day, when I joined a gathering crowd, he missed.)

'As I was ready to swing,' Palmer said of that first afternoon, 'I saw Gary standing there looking back. I thought about him for a moment. You know, I wanted to hit a good shot.'

'That's it! That's it!' Player told me in the locker room. 'He always knew how to share a moment of triumph, yours or his. Sometimes in life, it can be very hard to find someone to share your moments of triumph. I loved it when Jack and Arnie were partners. I hated it when they got so competitive, too competitive. But I knew they were both very good men. I just waited the cold spell out.'

According to Nicklaus's recollection, not Palmer's, the two started going their own ways after tying in that US Open at Oakmont in 1962.

'Before the play-off,' Nicklaus said, 'Arnie came up to me in the locker room and asked, "Would you like to split the prize money?" What was it, $9,000?'

'I did?' Palmer blinked.

'Yes, you did,' Nicklaus said, standing fast. 'I took it as a gesture made to a young kid. I will never forget it. *He* obviously has.'

They didn't split the money.

On the golf course, Palmer and Nicklaus competed so personally that, especially when they were paired together, they occasionally lost sight of the rest of the field. 'That happened a lot,' Nicklaus said. 'When two guys spend that much time together, their competitive juices flow. They try to whip each other.' In the Open at Chicago's Medinah course in 1975, either of them could have won, probably should have won. (Lou Graham beat John Mahaffey in a play-off.)

Palmer and Nicklaus were paired together in the final round. In the interview tent afterward, Nicklaus was bemoaning the closing three holes so pitifully that Palmer finally spoke up.

'Why don't you just sashay your ass back out there,' he said, 'and play them over?'

Nicklaus looked stunned, slapped. Quickly Palmer tossed a muscular forearm across Nicklaus's scalded neck and they both attempted to laugh. After that, to everyone but the public, the friction between them was plain to see. Off the tour, they competed even more personally. When both started carving their initials into mountainsides, each was loath to commend the other's architectural creations. Over the table, they damned their rival's courses with the faintest praise. Under it, they staged another shin-kicking contest that left them both black and blue.

In the manner of Bobby Jones at Augusta, each hoped to make an institution out of a signature course, Palmer at Bay Hill in Orlando, Florida, Nicklaus at Muirfield Village in Dublin, Ohio. While both are worthy courses and elite tournaments, neither is what their creators dreamed. For years, they snubbed each other's parties.

The pettiness that grew up between them found an illustration in the insignia on the pockets of Nicklaus-brand shirts, a Golden Bear. 'Why,' Palmer would enquire of a sportswriter, pinching the fabric and the skin underneath, 'are you wearing that yellow pig?' Quietly, the bear was redrawn into a less ambiguous shape.

'We didn't always see eye to eye on everything,' Nicklaus admitted, 'but there's one thing I'll always be proud of. In the important matters, when it came to the Tour and the game of golf, we always stood together. We didn't do everything perfectly. You try for perfection in golf, but you never get there. Not even close.'

As Palmer edged into his 60s, and Nicklaus his 50s, they turned back toward each other. Neither knows who turned first. 'We've gone out of our way to renew our friendship,' Nicklaus said, 'to play practice rounds routinely, to have dinners together again.' And to be partners again in team events.

At the Tradition, a senior tournament, Palmer knocked Nicklaus over by asking him to look at his swing. 'We've played for more than 30 years,' Jack said, 'and that's the first time he ever asked me. I was flattered by it, but he must really be desperate.'

Palmer said, 'My nature is to compete. It always has been and it always will be. Jack had nothing to do with that except he was there a lot. For ten years in a row, I had a chance to win the Open.' He turned to Nicklaus and said, 'You won them, but I had a chance.'

Forgetting they weren't alone, or maybe remembering they were, they returned in spirit to old battlefields such as Baltusrol. 'If you make that one at fourteen, if I miss that one at twelve, we're tied,' one of them said, I forget which one. They *were* tied. They always were tied. They always will be. As they slipped past 70 and 60, Arnie shot his age one day and trimmed Jack in a *Shell's Wonderful World of Golf* TV match. Just for the day, Palmer could putt again. 'He kicked my butt,' Nicklaus said in front of him.

'I want to congratulate Jack,' Arnie responded with an impish smile, 'on designing such a wonderful course.' (They had co-designed it.)

'When we're all together now, we still have the needle out,' said Player, who helped Shell with the play-by-play. 'We still compete like hell. But we know now that we love each other, and that we always did.'

Palmer's first professional victory was the Canadian Open, just about the only blue ribbon that eluded Nicklaus. In the immediate aftermath of peace, a Canadian journalist asked Jack if he would be returning to the tournament at Glen Abbey. Nicklaus replied, 'My wife says she's going to keep sending me back there until I get it right.'

To which Palmer enquired innocently, 'Are you sure she's talking about golf?'

THREE

In the summer of 1978, the same week Affirmed out-duelled Alydar to win the Belmont Stakes and the Triple Crown, I kidnapped Nancy Lopez in Cincinnati.

She was 21. It was her rookie year on tour, but already she had won five tournaments, including three in a row, and would run the streak to four in Ohio and to five ultimately. Coming to the LPGA Championship, she was taking her first ride on the national merry-go-round and enjoying it.

I had called the tournament office to see if I could interview her and was told to wait for the general press conference. I decided to pick her up at the airport instead.

'I have a confession to make,' I said in the car. 'I'm not with the tournament. I write a column for the *Cincinnati Enquirer.*' She was very nice about it. She didn't scream.

Nancy had flown in from Cleveland, where she had kept appointments with her agent and her orthodontist, equally numbing experiences. Earlier, in Reading, Pennsylvania, she had joined Tom Watson at an exhibition for Easter Seals. 'He's cute,' she said. 'Tom told everyone that if I beat him, he'd retire. I was a little worried about it. We were tied for a long time.'

She laughed easily. 'I know,' she said. 'I have to watch that. When I laugh, I can't swing a club.' And she cried easily, too. Recalling the Easter Seals kids, she said, 'To be walking around on a beautiful golf course on a beautiful day, I feel so lucky. I haven't thought much about winning three in a row. You have to go on. You can't say, "I'm great", and all that. I haven't really realised it yet. I don't know if I ever will.'

If memory can be trusted, she had a long-standing boyfriend named Ron and a suave, not to say, legendary, caddie named Roscoe. Roscoe Jones. (One isn't likely to forget a name like that.) But her life was uncharted. 'There are a lot of things in life more exciting than golf,' she said. 'I would like to get married, for one. But I don't think I could cope with it just yet. I remember in high school, guys would ask me, "Why do you have to go hit golf balls? Why don't you come to lunch with me?"'

At lunch with me (later that week), Hall of Famer Carol Mann predicted Lopez would marry the first tall, handsome stranger who smiled at her. His name was Tim Melton. He was a television sportscaster in Hershey, Pennsylvania, the chocolate town where their eyes met near the end of Nancy's streak. They moved to the very golf course where Lopez and I were heading. The Meltons' neighbours at the Jack Nicklaus Golf Center included Reds pitcher Tom Seaver and third baseman Ray Knight, and their wives.

Neither the lightning-bolt marriage nor the Cincinnati winters turned out to be a good fit for Nancy. Inside and out, she needed a warmer environment to keep her spirit up and her weight down. Partly to head off temptation, she talked Melton into moving with the tour to its new headquarters in Houston. But, God having a sense of humour, the temptation, in the person of Knight, was traded to the Astros. Nancy and Ray eventually married.

When we reached the golf course, she went almost immediately to the practice tee where, looking back, the line-up was unbelievable: Patty Berg, Mickey Wright, Kathy Whitworth, JoAnne Carner, Donna Caponi Young, Judy Rankin, all in a row. In the slot next to glamour girl Marlene

Hagge, Wimbledon and US Nationals tennis champion Althea Gibson was hitting fairway woods.

The first eminent black woman in two professional sports had left tennis for golf because, as she said, 'It's nice to win trophies, but you can't eat them.'

Gibson never did win an LPGA tournament or make all that much money playing golf. For years before her death in 2003, she would live as a recluse in East Orange, New Jersey, unavailable for comment on the successes of Serena and Venus Williams, who owe her so much. 'Have you heard the expression,' Althea asked me in the middle of a swing, 'that pioneers never reap the harvest?'

Sensing she could use a compliment, I told her, 'There's nothing wrong with that four-wood.'

'It's a three-wood,' she said.

When Nancy began hitting balls, only Wright turned away from her own preparations to watch. Mickey was 43, and the soreness in her feet was compelling her to play in tennis shoes, and sometimes bare feet, but she would open the tournament with a 69. Mickey was the queen. Strictly in golf terms, she still is.

But Nancy Lopez became the LPGA.

'She has the most poise and the most control,' Wright said, 'of any young player I've ever seen.'

In Tiger Woods fashion, Lopez won nine tournaments that year and eight the next. She was a big hitter and a beautiful putter. If she wasn't the best putter, she was the bravest. Maybe it's the same thing. To a sexist's eyes, she was the only woman in the world who got virtually every ball to the hole. She seemed to make more long putts than any other woman, or man, alive.

Speaking of sexism, this was an era when newspapers as respected as the *Los Angeles Times* and sportswriters as prominent as Jim Murray thought nothing of describing female athletes as Tugboat Annies and prison matrons, or of noting in print that the more feminine members of the LPGA Tour 'wore derbies and smoked cigars'.

When my friend John Hewig signed on as the tour's public relations director in the middle of the Lopez boom, commissioner Ray Volpe issued him two overriding commands: one, John should stand ready at a second's notice to stamp down the annual Amazons story; two, under no circumstances was he to have sex with any of the players. 'You've got the title for your book,' I told Hewig. '*Whatever You Do, Don't Sleep with the Lesbians*'.

But, thanks to Nancy, the image of the tour softened. The antidote to all of those oversize shorts and floppy hats was just her smile. Like the Nancy in Sinatra's song, she had that laughing face, set off by those eyes as dark as a panther's that, in the heat of the fight, just jumped off the television screen. At any weight, she was attractive. And she didn't say, 'I'm great', and all that. She didn't realise it yet. She never did.

In the middle of the tournament, I went to New York to see Affirmed win by a nose and returned to find Nancy leading by five lengths. Bob Trumpy, the Bengals' tight end, caught me up. 'You haven't missed any drama,' he said. 'Watching her is like watching Johnny Unitas in his prime.'

With a 13-under-par total of 275, easily a record for the LPGA Championship, Nancy won by six strokes to earn what now seems a measly $22,500. Judy Rankin said, 'They've got the wrong person on TV playing Wonder Woman.'

Trumpy asked me, 'What great athlete does she remind you of?'

I couldn't think of one then, but I can now: Jack Dempsey.

Red Smith used to tell this story: on the eve of a title fight, Dempsey, many years retired, was entertaining the writers in his Broadway restaurant when a fellow walked in off the street and said, 'Jack, I'm from Toledo, Ohio. I saw you beat Jess Willard there in 1919.'

'The hell you did!' Dempsey bellowed. 'Come join us! Have a drink!'

After sitting silently, happily, through several rounds of stories, the man from Toledo got up to leave. 'Thanks a lot, Jack,' he said, shaking hands, 'and I hope you knock that guy's block off tomorrow night.'

As the man walked out the door, Dempsey said softly, 'He thinks I'm still the champion.'

I think Nancy Lopez is still the champion. In fact, I know she is.

FOUR

About to be a junior in high school, I caddied in the 1961 Eastern Open for a Baltimore amateur who, with my help, easily missed the cut. Nevertheless, I lingered the rest of the week, still in uniform, since my only pass was the caddies' T-shirt stamped 'Eastern Open' on the front with 'Mr Boh' (the moustachioed mascot of National Bohemian beer) on the back. Doug Sanders won. Ken Venturi lost. Most important, I made $30.

This was at Pine Ridge, a new public course north of the city of Baltimore. Earlier, Pine Ridge pro Johnny Bass had called over to the Country Club of Maryland, to a flinty Scot named Andy Gibson, requesting two caddies to serve the mayor and three others in a ceremonial first foursome. That day I drew Bass, who would call me to the tournament, and sportswriter John Steadman, who would become my friend.

John just made it to auld lang syne, through two rough years of cancer, and died later on 1 January 2001, at 73. He was the most sentimental newspaperman in Baltimore. But Steadman was hard-bitten enough not to expect too much of the players. 'Milton Gross thought the players were all his friends,' he told me once, referring to a syndicated sports columnist in New York. 'None of them came to his funeral.'

Steadman was most closely associated with professional football, the beloved Colts of Johnny Unitas, Gino Marchetti and Lenny Moore (although John would probably start with Buddy Young, Jim Mutscheller and Bert Rechichar). But golf wasn't far down his list, and he was a regular at the Masters.

Maybe because it is one of those unchanging places, or maybe because it is spring, the Masters is a stop where you actually do stop. Looking around the press room, the first thing you see every year seems to be who's gone or going.

Anyone who hung around Steadman long enough, sooner or later, was bound to be trapped in a heartwarming column, and my number came up in the late '80s. He invited me back to the Country Club of Maryland, my old den of iniquity, and sprung Andy Gibson on me.

Gibson, who had seemed ancient when I was a boy, was long retired and hadn't taught or even played in quite a while. But he came out of retirement that day with us and, although he was 80, his swing hadn't changed. I was back in the glen shagging balls.

The caddie house, still grafted to the tailbone of the pro shop, was smaller and less toxic than I remembered. It still held the smoky aromas of the adult caddies from Sparrows Point: Wesley, Morgan, Jockey, Howser, O'Hara, One-Armed Duke and especially Smitty, a well-barbered ne'er-do-well who smelled of disappointment and Bay Rum and who kept two worn baseball mitts and a mildewed Rawlings ball lodged in an elbow of the propane tank out back. Chained and locked bicycles weren't safe in that yard, but no one disturbed the props that Smitty pulled out near the end of the day to pretend he still had sons.

Our fourth was Lou Sleater, a good-hitting left-handed pitcher for the Orioles in the '50s, so the mood was perfect. The ghosts playing all around us included George Rogers, the brilliantined MC of *Shell's Wonderful World of Golf*; Paul Richards, the sulphurous old catcher and manager from Waxahachee, Texas; and a local broadcasting legend, Bailey Goss.

'Have you ever been in the clubhouse before?' Gibson asked afterward at a dining room table. It was a fair question.

I told him, 'The caddies didn't spend that much time socialising with the Vanderbilts, but you brought me in once to see a blown-up photograph of the 13th green. I was in the picture, attending the pin.'

Just like in the movies, our eyes went from the table to the wall beside us, and there it was. Gibson lived to be 87.

Steadman should have. By the way, Unitas, Mutscheller, Moore, Tom Matte, Art Donovan – all of them – came to his funeral.

Not long after Gibson died, I returned home from a trip to find a large package on my porch. As soon as I saw 'Lou Sleater' in the corner of the address label, I knew what it was, a bequest. Steadman's fingerprints were all over it, too.

Hanging on the wall of my spelling room now, it isn't just a photograph. It's more like a window. Every day, looking out the window at the 13th green, I can see Wesley, Morgan, Jockey, Howser, O'Hara, One-Armed Duke, Smitty, Mr Gibson, Mr Rogers, Mr Richards, Mr Goss, Mr Bass, Mr Steadman, everybody.

5

The Canary That Won the Derby

In Salty Bar Harbor, Maine, where Lithuanian emigrants imagined they could taste a Baltic breeze, Shirley was a common boy's name at the beginning of the twentieth century. Except to feel slightly sorry for a girl named Shirley Johnson, Shirley Povich scarcely gave it a thought until, in the middle of a 70-year run as the sports editor of the *Washington Post*, he received the most stupefyingly grand if singularly undeserved honor of his life. Right there between Louise Pound and Hortense Powdermaker, Shirley was listed in *Who's Who in American Women*.

'For years I've known it's no longer a man's world,' he said in humble appreciation. 'I'm glad to be officially listed on the winning side.' Although red-faced editors dropped him the following year ('like I'd married a stripper or something,' he grumbled, 'the snobs'), Shirley maintained his association with Edna Ferber, Dorothy Thompson and Mary Roberts Rinehart via his membership in the League of American Penwomen.

'Has sex been any handicap to you in the journalism profession?' he was asked in a questionnaire.

'None at all,' he responded honestly.

'How do you get along with the men in your office?'

'I just try to be one of the boys.'

'This is McSorley's Pool Hall. Did you leave a hat here last night?'

'If there's a head in it,' Red said, 'send it over.' Russell was the most impeccably dressed and parsimonious-looking gentleman in the entire newspaper profession, and the very last man you'd peg for a dedicated practical joker.

Checking into a hotel late at night, a bunch of us were stuck behind a plush-bottomed woman who, after taking twice as much time as anyone else, spent five extra minutes emphasising the importance of her 7.30 wake-up call. When his turn came, Fred requested a 7.15 call. He awoke only long enough to call Miss Plushbottom and say, 'This is your 7.30 wake-up call. Get your fat ass out of bed!'

Murray was the most celebrated humourist in our group. In Zaire, Jim told Ali, 'I'd like to borrow your body for around ten days, because there are about five women I'd like to nail and about five guys I'd like to beat the hell out of.' Near the end of his life, resting with Sherrod in the stairwell of another ballpark, Murray said, 'Blackie, you know something? One day they're going to find me dead on the steps of some damn stadium and people are going to say, "He wouldn't have had it any other way." I want you to tell them for me, "That's bullshit."'

We all knew Secretariat was a pretty fair horse.

'How did he work this morning, Charlie?' Red asked old Charlie Hatton of the *Daily Racing Form*, the man who invented the Triple Crown. (Charlie had grown weary of spelling out which three races Gallant Fox won in 1930.) 'The trees swayed,' Hatton answered beautifully. But we were pulling for a horse called Sham because we had just left Claiborne Farm in Paris, Kentucky, and our notebooks were bulging with a column about Sham and a man named Bull Hancock. As always, we were rooting for our columns. (Or plinths, as Red called them in pidgin Greek. 'Give us this day,' he'd pray, 'our daily plinth.')

Hancock, the master of Claiborne, had recently died of cancer. He was a hardboot who had studied genetics at Princeton and bourbon in Bourbon County. During a fabled career, Bull had bred many eminent thoroughbreds for Ogden Phipps and other aristocratic customers but had never saddled a Derby horse of his own. Sham was going to be that.

A son of Pretense might only naturally be called Sham, but the name didn't suit him. He was a dark, leggy, elegant bay who would ride alongside history instead of into it. He would be the long fly ball caught on the warning track, the curling putt that lipped out in the end, the last-quarter touchdown drive that died at the one-yard line.

Inheritance taxes regularly turn the thoroughbred industry inside out. Upon Hancock's death, all of Claiborne's racing stock had to be sold so that all of the breeding stock could be kept. The Hancocks begged the executors to make an exception of Bull's pet, but they wouldn't. Sham had to go. He bore someone else's silks at Churchill.

Bull sired two boys: Seth, the Good Son, and Arthur Boyd Hancock III, the Black Sheep. Young Arthur was six years older than Seth, 29 to 23, when their father died. But Arthur didn't act it. As a small child, spurred on by his grandmother's gift of a ukulele, he fell in love with twangy music. In his teens, the ukulele morphed into a guitar. Arthur brilliantined his hair and began to list noticeably toward the Grand Ole Opry.

His friends called him 'Elvis'. His father called him 'the Canary'. In the Lexington papers, Bull read about his long-haired son leaping up on the stage at Joyland Park and duckwalking like Chuck Berry to Little Enis and the Tabletoppers' rendition of 'Johnny B. Goode'. When he wasn't picking his guitar and writing sentimental lyrics, Arthur was picking fights in bars and sleeping it off in drunk tanks. A champion swimmer at Vanderbilt, he had enough air and strength to pop the police department's breathalyser balloons, and this became one of his favourite pastimes.

Arthur and Bull eventually had a knock-down, drag-out fistfight. Six foot four or not, Arthur was the one who was knocked down. Still, he loved his father, and while only his father seemed to know it, Arthur also loved the bluegrass. Not long before he died, Bull quietly leased Arthur a little hundred-acre spread near Claiborne to run and learn on his own. 'I was like you once,' Bull murmured. The place was called Stone Farm. Away from the others, they talked about the industry, about the fruit flies Bull had studied at Princeton. Among the fruit flies – Bull wanted Arthur never to forget – the 'complete outcrosses' had the most vitality. A thoroughbred is a complete outcross if no name appears more than once in the first four generations of his family tree. (Just to give you an idea of how inbred racing is, consider that all 16 horses in the 2003 Kentucky Derby were related to Northern Dancer.)

Arthur presumed he would be the new master of Claiborne, but on the harrumphed advice of Bull's old friend and client, Phipps, the executors passed over the Canary for diligent young Seth. As Arthur wandered off into the wilderness, Seth immediately syndicated Secretariat for a record $6.8 million ($190,000 a breeding share) a full ten weeks before the Kentucky Derby. In effect, Seth placed the biggest wager of all on the race and on the entire Triple Crown series, and he won big.

Sham would have won every other Derby run at a mile and a quarter. Over that stretch of ground, Secretariat and Sham were the first two horses to come home in under two minutes. (Only Monarchos in 2001 has done it since, slower than both of them.) Slammed into the starting gate at the bell, Sham ran a huge race with a fat lip to finish two and a half lengths behind.

He was second in the Preakness as well, again by two and

a half. Smith, who may have prized Preaknesses even above Derbys, wrote, 'I can never forget Ridan and Greek Money coming down the stretch in 1962 so close together that Manny Ycaza was riding both horses. Rooting for Native Dancer, I shivered with fear when Jamie K. gave chase to the grey in 1953. Of all of them, I thought Whirlaway's Preakness would always be the most vivid in memory. When Whirlaway turned on the heat, you could hear a frying sound. But, trying to watch Secretariat, I couldn't hold my binoculars steady.'

Then, a quarter of a century between Triple Crowns, Secretariat and Sham went loping ahead of just a five-horse field at Belmont Park. In the backstretch, hidden by the tote board, Sham finally despaired. From ten lengths astern, Braulio Baeza on Twice a Prince and Angel Cordero on My Gallant could actually see Sham's heart breaking. They glanced over at each other in unabashed astonishment. Sham's legs were splaying apart. He was swimming instead of running. He was crying out in distress. The sound couldn't be heard in the din of Belmont Park. Secretariat was alone on the homestretch.

'I'm gonna get second, man!' Baeza shouted.

'You gotta beat me!' cried Cordero. They picked up their whips. As no one remembers, Twice a Prince did get second – a full 31 lengths behind the winner. Sham came home dead last, 45 lengths to oblivion. He never raced again.

When Secretariat died 16 years later, the world sent flowers by the truckload. He was buried in the company of Johnstown, Round Table, Bold Ruler and a lot of other horses with names like plucked harp strings.

Sham died four years after that, still dispensing sexual favours for $3,500 per live foal. Without much ceremony, he was buried in Lexington near a horse of mysterious accomplishment named Brent's Prince. They were the only two in the graveyard. No one sang songs or drank toasts to Sham.

Just a few Mays after Secretariat's and Sham's illustrious campaign, I arrived once again at the Campbell House, and Red said to Murphy, 'Did you tell Tom about the bottle cap I won?'

'I didn't think it was my place,' Jack said.

'C'mon,' Red told me, 'let's take a walk.'

He was seventy then and had six years to live.

I was familiar with the expression 'bottle cap'. I knew it came from Stanley Woodward, the legendary sports editor of the *Herald Tribune*. I never knew Woodward, but he must have been something. Once, when the paper's owner ordered Stanley to trim the staff by two, he obediently fired himself and Red. (They went off together on a bender.) Presented with some early writing award, Red proudly propped it up on his desk in the newsroom. 'Are you going to stare at that bottle cap all day?' sneered Woodward. Casually, Red slipped it into a drawer.

'I've won the Pulitzer Prize,' he told me as we walked.

'Great!'

'It's not that great. The *New York Times* passes them around.'

During the '50s, when the *Herald Trib* kicked the *Times* up and down the block every morning just for light exercise, Red made a Spanish omelette out of a nice, pedestrian *Times* columnist named Arthur Daley. During this period, Red was on a train when his wife returned from the club car with coffee, a newspaper and a cheery question.

'What's the last thing in the world you can ever imagine happening?' she asked Red.

Not meaning to be mean, just being as quick and funny as always, Smith replied, 'Arthur Daley winning the Pulitzer Prize.'

'Oh, Red,' she said, 'but he did.'

Smith was hardly a vainglorious man. To hear him tell it,

all of the Grantland Rices and Joe Palmers of his youth were better than he. 'I was always the third-to-the-last guy out of the press box,' he'd say, 'and it didn't console me to see Allison Danzig and Westbrook Pegler still writing. Because I knew Danzig would be twice as long and Pegler would be twice as good.' An excruciatingly slow writer, Red would turn to me and whisper, 'I hope I'm not getting any blood on you.' Or I'd turn to him and say, 'Are you on the 18th hole yet?' He'd sigh and reply, 'I'm struggling up the 17th fairway, but my ball is out of bounds.' If it wrote hard, though, it read easy. He knew he was good. In fact, he could list the things he did well. 'I can make a martini, I can write a plinth . . .' And he was ashamed that Daley's award hurt him so. But it did.

He knew I knew it. That's why we were walking. 'I always promised myself I'd refuse the Pulitzer,' Red said as we circled the Campbell House on its impeccable lawn, 'but I've decided that 70-year-old crocks who are bitter are boring. You can't tell anybody I've won it, by the way. I'm not supposed to know. Scotty Reston leaked it to me. I'm going to go back to the office and Abe Rosenthal's going to spring it on me and I'm going to say, "Oh, dear diary, what a break." But I want you to know it doesn't mean a thing to me. I'm going to toss it in a closet.'

Not too long after that, Murphy died too young. He ended up a ballpark in San Diego for a while. (Now he's a statue in front of it, walking his old black Labrador retriever, Abe of Spoon River.) Jack would have hooted at all of that.

Red wasn't up to going to the funeral. 'Be my legs, will you?' he said over the phone. 'Take notes.'

I took them furiously. Archie Moore, Don Coryell and Al Davis were among the speakers. In the early '60s, loving San Diego but needing to know if he could have played the Palace, Murphy queried the great and benevolent *New Yorker* editor

William Shawn, to see if Shawn would consider a profile on Moore. Tersely, Shawn responded, 'Joe Liebling handles our boxing quite well, thank you.'

Jack persisted. 'I'm a huge A.J. Liebling fan,' he wrote, 'but I've been around Archie for his whole career, and there are some good stories to tell.'

Promising nothing except to look at it, Shawn said, 'Start a piece. Send me 10,000 words.' Jack wrote it hard, mailed it and waited. Eventually, a telegram arrived. It thrilled him more than any gift he ever received, and it quelled his doubts forever. Three words: 'Finish it. Shawn.' The headline on Jack's *New Yorker* piece was 'The Mongoose'.

Davis, the Oakland Raiders' ageing Fonzie, sporting the last duck-tail haircut in Western civilisation, spotted Barron Hilton in the pews and began telling old American Football League stories. Murphy was the one who talked Hilton into relocating the Los Angeles Chargers to San Diego. Al used to run with Barron's brother, Nicky, who didn't mind talking up the fledging AFL at Rotary Clubs and Cub Scout meetings, but he hated the inevitable way he was introduced, as Elizabeth Taylor's first husband. 'Until finally,' Davis told the congregation, 'someone got up and said, "Now I'd like to introduce a man who once made $100,000 in the baseball business, Conrad Hilton Jr."'

'Nicky ran to the podium, he was so thrilled.

'He said, "I want to thank this gentleman for such a wonderful introduction, the best one I've ever received. It's correct in every particular, except: it was not baseball, it was football; it was not $100,000, it was $1,000,000; it was not made, it was lost; and, it was not me, it was my brother."' I can still hear Red laughing on the phone. He died on a Friday night in January, nine days before a Super Bowl. I was closing a cover story at *Time* on Joe Montana when a researcher peeked in the door and asked, 'What year did Red Smith win the Pulitzer Prize?'

'I don't know, five or six years ago. Why?'

'I'm doing the Milestone on him.'

That following spring, Lexington felt empty. Louisville wasn't any better. Sentimentally, I latched on to a horse named Cassaleria, another misbegotten son of Pretense. One of Cassaleria's first bobbling steps after birth tumbled him into a fence post and poked out his left eye, leaving a sorry-looking, fleshed-over socket. A one-eyed colt with claustrophobia, he was the solitary member of the '20/20 Stable' (slogan: 'Thine eye has seen the glory'). Sham's little brother had earned his trip to Churchill Downs by winning the El Camino Real Derby at Bay Meadows in San Mateo, California. After the race, it was discovered that his eye had been entirely covered over by mud. He had run blind.

Cassaleria finished 13th in Louisville. He never seemed to be leading with the correct foot. The winner was an equally unlikely colt, a 21–1 shot that went into the first turn in last place and passed 18 horses to win. He was a grey named Gato del Sol, flying the colours of Stone Farm.

The Canary had won the Derby.

'I want to dedicate it to my dad,' said Arthur Hancock. 'He taught me all I know.'

By the way, Gato del Sol was a complete outcross.

A few years later, crusty old Ogden Phipps, the man who had kinged Seth and dismissed Arthur, came up with a super horse who was being mentioned in the same breath with Secretariat. For all of his success in breeding and racing, Phipps had never won the Kentucky Derby and looked sure to do it with Easy Goer. But a horse named for a song lyric, Sunday Silence, edged Easy Goer in both the Derby and, in as heart-stopping a race as has ever been run, the Preakness. Although they changed places in the Belmont, Sunday Silence settled the score for all time in the Breeders' Cup.

Plucking a guitar, Arthur sang the song he wrote for his

horse: 'We all need a guiding hand to help us now and then / Here comes Sunday Silence again.'

Arthur became a breeder of renown. 'Look at that little foal,' he said one morning at the farm. 'If he can't run, I'm not my father's son.' That colt would be named Fusaichi Pegasus. He'd win the Derby, too. Phyllis Smith asked me to go through the mountain of mail to see whose condolences she should personally answer. 'Does Richard Nixon's qualify?' I asked Red's wife, holding up Nixon's letter. (When it came to abhorring Nixon, Red was practically the first one in line.) 'Oh, Lord, I guess so,' she said. After a few hours in Red's barn in New Canaan, Connecticut, I got up to stretch and explore. In a little closet off his office, amid all of his fishing junk, there was a stack of wooden plaques, a screwdriver and a pile of metal curlicues. He was prying the faces off his bottle caps and using the backs for firewood. In the corner, covered with dust, was the Pulitzer Prize.

On the eve of a Garden fight, a cocktail tribute was begun at New York's Yale Club and resumed at Runyon's bar for a sportswriter who drank himself to death at 47. Newspaper reporters, TV broadcasters, magazine editors, singers, actors and authors (Bill Murray and Kurt Vonnegut, no less) toasted their friend Pete Axthelm for, in the phrase of several of the speakers, 'living life on his own terms'.

In racetrack terms, someone noted colourfully, he did the life in '47 and change'. For however many furlongs that represented, it was a good time. Lonesome songs by Willie Nelson filled the Yale Club. Runyonesque tales were recounted, such as the one about the Yale undergraduate who played poker through the night and then remembered he had to take the law boards that morning; who achieved a perfect score but went to Aqueduct Race Track instead of law school.

Ax had to shoot through Yale in a blink to make it to the dying *New York Herald Tribune* just under the wire. 'He had to be older than 47,' said the sportswriters when his obituary appeared. He had looked 47 for

20 years. The headline on most of the Axthelm obits was some variation of: 'TV Personality Dies'. His friends cringed at that, especially. He was a writer.

Highlights of Ax's NBC and ESPN reports were played for the sipping mourners. The tapes reminded everyone of just how wooden Ax usually was on television, although in an interview setting with the likes of street basketball legend Sam Drummer, he was himself.

'Which is the stronger feeling?' he asked Drummer. 'The good memories or what might have been?'

Axthelm courted TV for money and fame. Once, in a Super Bowl pre-game show, he portrayed himself, the football tout, in a mock episode of *Cheers*. Awaiting his cue to enter the sitcom saloon, Ax peered through a Tiffany door at Diane Chambers, Sam Malone, Carla, Norm and Cliff. 'You're still a *Newsweek* writer,' the soundman heard Pete whisper. 'You've just fallen down a rabbit hole.' Even after leaving *Newsweek* a couple of years before he died, Axthelm essentially remained a *Newsweek* writer. The day I went to *Time* magazine to be his counterpart, Ax pulled me aside in Runyon's. 'You'd pick it up quickly on your own,' he said, 'but I've been a newsmagazine guy for 12 years and I can tell you some of the ins and outs if you want to know.'

I listened to him for several hours and everything he said helped. 'You're pretty generous to a competitor,' I signed off with a laugh.

'Aren't we friends?' he replied.

In a Super Bowl press box, as the Raiders blocked a Redskins punt, Ax let out a whoop. He turned to me penitently and whispered, 'I apologise, that was very unprofessional. But I've got $4,000 on the Raiders.'

He relentlessly backed the Raiders, the Dolphins and horses of a certain sinew: Thirty-Six Red, Majestic Prince, Houston. Ax was what the handicappers call 'a beader', a conformation specialist. Before he bet, he liked to check out the legs in the paddock. (I was there looking at legs, too.) In the horse readings at the Yale Club, all of Pete's subjects seemed to be reaching down into their muscles and heart.

There were very few tears at the Yale Club, a lot of 'He did it his way.'

Some in the congregation were sore at columnist Jimmy Breslin, who knew Pete Axthelm before he was Pete Axthelm and reacted angrily both at the death and at the rhapsody around it.

Breslin was furious with Ax. He didn't come to the party. I think he may have been Pete's best friend.

6

A Brief Pause: Work Going on at the Time

THE SKY OPENED

On the only day when people who don't care about horse racing care about horse racing – the first Saturday in May – a red stallion with three white stockings finally reached the gates of heaven.

He had foundered with laminitis in the winter, his 19th winter, which is a genteel way of saying an infection filled his feet with so much pus that he had to lie down and die. By the time 300 of his 1,300 pounds had been worried away, his humans took pity on him and shot a concentrated dose of barbiturate into his jugular vein, 'putting him down', as they say. Beyond the compassion it signalled, he was flattered by the syringe, because he knew it rendered him unrenderable. Neither rendering plants (glue factories) nor pet food companies will accept horse carcasses medicated this way. Reportedly, the next stop is Lion Country Safari, although the chestnut with the three white stockings wondered if this wasn't just an old mare's tale. Being dead, he felt nothing when they cut off his testicles for examination (not a pleasant event, even for an out-of-body experience), along with, one by one, the sickly hooves that had carried him through the fastest Kentucky Derby and the sweetest Triple Crown. Next, they removed his heart, which, while entirely healthy, was more than twice the size of the average thoroughbred's, much bigger than any heart the pathologists had ever seen. Ordinarily, the head would be the only other part they would bury. Prepared to go out like Sydney Carton (and, being something of a baseball fan, rooting for the hide to go to Haiti), he was quietly moved when the humans reassembled his pieces and interred him whole in the horses' graveyard under a small white stone that read simply:

SECRETARIAT
1970–1989

Across the way was Swale, whose inscription could not have been more pathetic (1981–1984), alongside Round Table, who lived 30 years longer. Down the lane, as the stones grew progressively mossier, resided Johnstown, who won the Derby in 1939, next to Gallant Fox, who took the Triple Crown in 1930. He was the only Triple Crown winner to sire a Triple Crown winner, the misbegotten Omaha, who flopped so miserably at stud that he closed out his career fathering cavalry horses at a remount station in Douglaston, Wyoming. Further along rested Princequillo, the maternal grandsire of the red horse with the three white stockings. What a character. A veteran of the air war over Britain, the prince was conceived in France, born in England, spirited away to Ireland and shipped through a U-boat ambush to America. Red's father, Bold Ruler, was there also. The mother, Somethingroyal, ended up alone under a holly tree and white pine, next to a little dogs' graveyard in Virginia. His own offspring were on the red horse's mind. General Assembly finished second to the famous

Spectacular Bid in the 1979 Derby, and Lady's Secret was the 1986 Horse of the Year. But the uncomfortable truth was, he never duplicated himself in accomplishment or appearance; and the overwhelming sadness was, he nearly did. After an ultimate union with the Derby-winning filly Genuine Risk, he waited and waited, and could scarcely believe the cruel bulletin that made its way to him pasture by pasture straight from the horses' mouths: a stillborn colt, a chestnut with three white stockings.

The red horse seldom contemplated human beings and their similar sorrows. But today, Derby Day, he thought he should. He used to believe they were God's dumbest creatures. If a horse is amenable to being ridden, people deem him smart. If the horse doesn't care to have a disagreeable little brigand on his back beating his behind with a leather bat, they consider him stupid. When you are stabled in a 16-by-16-foot box all day, is it weird behaviour to want to bite a smelly little groom whose principal duty seems to be to yank a chain that is never taken out of your mouth?

But gradually he came around to a certain appreciation, if not a complete understanding, of the relationship between horses and humans. He eventually worked it all out in the head they hadn't chopped off and the heart they reinstalled in his chest.

Except in rare circumstances, horses aren't necessary anymore. Humans may desire one but they don't really require one, not in a practical sense. Inclined (like most male animals) to explain everything in relation to himself, the big chestnut decided humans go on needing horses, valuing them, loving them, because such feelings have been bred into people.

A century and a half ago, the horse meant survival. In America, the riders and the horses won the West together. Horses fetched doctors from remote villages. The connection between horses and men was so umbilical that thieves who misunderstood its importance had to be hanged. Horses carried mail and pulled trains. Not as an abstract, as a concrete measurement, horsepower endures. When all of this came clear to him, the sky opened and he began, like a rolling drum, to pick up his sore feet. Seeing horse shapes in the clouds, he made for them like Pegasus. He passed Bayard, who had a hoof in beating Charlemagne, and took off after Bucephalus, who carried Alexander. On the run now, he reached General Robert E. Lee's old friend Traveler, trotting alongside Little Sorrel, who bled with Stonewall Jackson, and he didn't break stride. Overtaking Man o'War, Whirlaway, Ruffian, Seabiscuit, Nashua, Swaps, Carry Back and Citation, he kept getting faster and faster. The drum roll became thunder. He was whole again and himself, a tremendous machine on the homestretch at Belmont, a living flame in the sky.

In the distance, a speck became a dot became a blot became a horse. Because tears work like glasses for horses and humans, he could make out the miniature figure miles before it made him out.

It was a little red colt with three white stockings.

COOL PAPA BELL

Maybe because his visitor was from Washington, DC, Cool Papa acted especially proud of the Griffith Stadium photograph, although his picture collection included every big-league ballpark he had ever graced, always when the main tenants were away.

In the Griffith snapshot, no players were visible, just grass and dirt and an outfield fence plastered with advertisements for lumber and liniment. When Cool Papa first brought it to his wife, Clara, he asked her, if she could, to imagine he was somewhere in the picture. 'Imagine me young,' he said.

'Imagine me 24.'

Subsequently, he located a photo of his actual self sliding into a real base at Griffith Stadium. But Clara preferred the imaginary one. Therefore, so did Cool Papa Bell.

James Thomas Bell played professional baseball from 1922 to 1946 for the St Louis Stars, the Pittsburgh Crawfords, the Detroit Wolves, the Kansas City Monarchs, the Chicago American Giants, the Memphis Red Sox and the inappropriately named Homestead Grays, who rattled around Pittsburgh for a number of forlorn seasons before meandering to the District of Columbia. Bell also served several winter-league teams throughout Latin America, along with a variety of barnstorming caravans trailing county fairs and passing hats. In the Negro Leagues, teams never played more than three games a day. Pitchers seldom registered more than 30 starts a month. Cool Papa was a pitcher for a time, then a centre fielder. He was the ultimate centre fielder. In the company of Smokey Joe Williams, 'Cannonball' Dick Redding, Steel Arm Dickey, Mules Suttles, Buck Leonard, Josh Gibson, Judy Johnson and Satchel Paige, monickers were practically mandatory. Cool Papa earned his at 19 with just the trace of a smile, looking in for the sign, before striking out the great Oscar Charleston in the clutch. 'He's taking it cool,' whispered someone on the bench. Manager Bill Gatewood added 'Papa' for panache.

To the white sportswriters who frequently dropped in on Bell during the 1980s, whenever the St Louis Cardinals were in the play-offs or World Series, Cool Papa retold his legend without bluster in a tidy house in an East St Louis, Illinois, neighbourhood about half as dire as the writers' descriptions. Well into his 70s, Bell listed a trifle to one side. But he 'jangled gently as he moved', just as Paige always prescribed, 'taking care to pacify the stomach with cool thoughts'.

'Cool Papa,' Satchel famously said, 'was so fast that he could turn off the light switch and jump into bed before the room got dark.'

Speeding between first and second base, Bell had to take care not to run into his own line drives. He was liable to score on his own bunt. Once, in Birmingham, where a catcher named Perkins had 'Thou Shalt Not Steal' stencilled across his chest protector, Cool Papa took off from first with a musical laugh. Just as Perkins's peg reached second base, Cool Papa slid into third. Next to Bell, the Baltimore Orioles' Paul Blair would play a distant centre field. Cool Papa patrolled so near to second base that he frequently tiptoed in for pick-off attempts. Overthrowing third one time in Memphis, he raced to the base, caught the carom off the dugout roof and completed the first '8–8' putout in history. 'A few guys living today saw it,' he said modestly. Cool Papa batted over .400 twice: his first season and his last. Never did he hit under .300. Creaky with arthritis near the end, he intentionally kept his plate appearances just below the qualifying level so that Monte Irvin could win the batting title. Jackie Robinson was coming and Irvin was young enough to follow him. 'That's the way we thought back then,' Bell said. 'When one made it to the major leagues, we all did.'

Of course, the technicality cost him a bonus that had been written into his contract. 'Well, you didn't win the title, did you?' said the black owner. 'Owners is owners,' Cool Papa said, 'whether they blue or green.' Josh Gibson was 'the black Babe Ruth', Buck Leonard 'the black Lou Gehrig'. But Cool Papa was a prototype. Maury Wills, Lou Brock, Rickey Henderson – they all came from him.

One day at Busch Stadium, Bell waited at the visitors' gate for Wills. 'Maybe you heard of me, Mr Wills, maybe not, it don't matter,' he said after introducing himself to the Dodger shortstop. 'But I'd like to help you. When you're on base, get your hitters to stand as deep as they can in the batter's box. That'll push the catcher back a little, get you another half-step.'

Wills was stunned. 'I would never have thought of it,' he

murmured as Cool Papa waved and walked away. That was the season Wills broke the base-stealing record.

Bell was a custodian at St Louis City Hall for nine years, a night watchman for twelve more. Then he retired with Clara, organising their year around an annual trip to Cooperstown, New York, to cheer the Willie Stargells and Joe Morgans, who entered the Hall of Fame through the front door. In later years, collectors flimflammed the Bells out of most of their mementos, although a few photographs were saved, including one of Griffith Stadium with nobody in the picture.

Clara died on an uncommonly mild morning in January. There was just enough strength left in Cool Papa's heart to take care of everything that needed taking care of. Then, on a Thursday night, he joined her.

He was 24.

A PURE GIFT

On a shimmering day in a simple gym, tambourines jingled, hands clapped, voices rang and eyes glistened in the sweet celebration of a gift. In South Africa, the Zulus say *sipho*. Gift. In English, we say Arthur Ashe. For half an afternoon, the Arthur Ashe Jr Athletic Center, one of his smaller endowments to the world, became a Baptist church with bleachers, a school assembly without proctors. The mood was right for a commencement exercise, a valedictory, a reunion, a homecoming, even a pep rally, just about everything but a funeral. In a pretty way, someone used the word 'home-going', too. The homegoing for a 'moral giant', a 'quiet soul amid a noisy life', a 'beautiful black man', an 'elegant tennis player', a 'freedom fighter', a 'champion of life' (and a hero of living), 'gracious', 'righteous' and 'non-negotiably' true. Their old friend – no, young friend – Arthur.

A governor, a couple of mayors and a cabinet member

spoke. Preachers and players followed, all of them hitting the corners. Near the back of the congregation sat Australian Rod Laver, still as orange as the aurora borealis. The Rocket wasn't a speaker, just a mourner. He flew all day and all night from Australia. He would fly all night and all day back. The best tennis player who ever lived had come to pay his respects to the best liver who ever played. The crowd of some 6,000 was more than predominantly black, but the white minority felt at ease and entirely comfortable, a slightly shameful irony. The green heating ducts and cream rafters duplicated the colours of Richmond's Maggie L. Walker High School, where Arthur started his classes but couldn't stay.

Among the missing mourners were his father, Arthur Robert Sr, his mother, Mattie Cunningham, and his original patron from the playgrounds, the suitably named Ronald Charity, who referred the littlest tennis player (in those days, the racket seemed to have hold of him) to Dr Walter 'Whirlwind' Johnson, a Lynchburg physician who became Ashe's Branch Rickey. Dr Johnson was there in spirit, possibly sitting next to Jackie Robinson.

So was Jim Crow, childhood companion to all black children of the South, and not just the South, who ran Ashe out of town and away to St Louis in the '50s when Arthur sought merely to play high school tennis. Not meanly or perversely – brightly and breezily – Ashe liked to recount that, upon his triumphant return to Richmond in the '60s, he was fêted at City Hall by the new mayor, Morrill Crowe. 'No relation,' Arthur would say.

Ashe imagined he was literally born on a playground, since his father served as guardian, caretaker and policeman at the largest public park for blacks in Richmond, Brookfield Park. Its centrepiece and symbol was a perpetually empty swimming pool drained by Ol' Jim to forestall any possibility of a black child and a white one ever making the same splash.

Ashe's father was a sturdy, blocky man, terrific with his hands, capable of constructing his own house from the floorboards up. Neither physically nor mechanically did young Arthur take after him. Rather, he was Mattie's boy, and she was terribly light and fragile – dreamy, too – though resolute at the same time.

Five years into her marriage, Mattie heard a doctor decree she could never have children. She gritted her teeth and changed doctors. After an operation, she conceived and delivered a tiny boy; then, four years or so later, a larger one. Twenty-one months after that, she died.

Arthur Jr was six. Arthur Sr didn't know how to tell him. Inside the house, they walked silently for a while, hand in hand, that incongruously large fist enveloping those incalculably delicate fingers. 'Mattie has had a stroke,' he said finally. 'Do you understand what that is? It's like a gift from God for someone who's in pain. It takes away the pain. That's the really good part. But, the sad part is, it also takes away the person. The glad part is that she goes straight to heaven.'

Of course there were tears in the boy's eyes, but no panic in his expression. 'Well, Daddy,' Arthur said like a miniature adult, 'as long as we're together, everything will be all right.'

Many years later, Arthur Sr was surrounded by a cordon of reporters following one of his son's tennis glories. When they asked him if he were ever prouder of Arthur Jr, he told the story of the little giant.

Ashe's daughter, Camera, happened also to be six. 'Camera, sweetheart . . .' New York mayor David Dinkins began to address her, but what can you say? Except that it's like a gift from God for someone who's in pain. It takes away the pain. That's the really good part. But, the sad part is, it also takes away the person. The glad part is that he goes straight to heaven.

Before Arthur could tell his father he had AIDS, they had

to walk around it a little bit like before. That kindly man was overcome not just with sorrow but also guilt. He blamed himself for Arthur's genes, for the heart attacks, the open-heart surgery and the tainted transfusion.

'I never once in my life talked back to my father,' Arthur said, 'until then. I told him not to take it that way. Didn't he know he had given me everything? He was a pure gift to all of us.' Arthur Sr died three years before his son, of a heart attack.

A pure gift to all of us. That's right. That's the way to take it.

7

Shoeless Pete

It was opening day of the 1972 World Series and, in the pre-game milling, all of the black players among the A's and Reds just wanted to touch Jackie Robinson. White haired and virtually blind, Robinson looked 20 years older than 53. Ten days later, he'd be dead.

Joe Morgan of Cincinnati, the same kind of second baseman as Robinson, was the only one who didn't address him, who continued playing catch on the sidelines until the call came for all of the non-uniformed personnel to leave the field.

At which point Morgan stepped up behind Jackie and, without identifying himself, leaned into Robinson's shoulder blades and whispered, 'Thank you.'

'You're welcome,' Robinson said without turning around. I followed Jackie as he walked through the dugout and up the ramp into the Reds clubhouse, where Jim Murray of the *Los Angeles Times* was standing. 'Jackie, it's Jim Murray,' Jim said when they touched.

'Oh, Jim,' Robinson answered, 'I wish I could see you again.'

'No, Jackie,' Murray said gently, 'I wish we could see you again.'

Pete Rose was taught to lie on his first day with the Cincinnati Reds when an executive with the club, Phil Seghi, thought 19 an unseemly age for a high school senior and suggested they say 17. That would forestall any questions about the year Rose had been kept back in school (tenth grade). Pete said fine. Anything for baseball was fine. When Rose was an especially little little-leaguer, drowning in the catcher's equipment, waving the ball in the hitters' faces, taunting them obnoxiously, 'Hey, batter, batter, batter,' his father struck a bargain with the manager: if Pete would be permitted to switch-hit, even in clutch situations, he would be left at home to play the games when the rest of the family went off on summer vacations.

As a matter of fact, Pete never set foot out of Cincinnati until the day he departed for the minor leagues.

His dad was a banker and a local sports legend, well known for playing halfback with the semi-pro Cincinnati Bengals at the Methuselan age of 42 and for not only sparring with World Featherweight Champion Freddie Miller but for holding his own. Pete adored his father. Until the very day the old man died, they were ferocious rivals in one-on-one basketball games. 'When I was young,' Pete said, 'people would stop me on the street to tell me I could never be what my father was.' He agreed with them completely.

Enos Slaughter of the St Louis Cardinals was the elder Rose's favourite ballplayer. Slaughter's hustle extended even to running out his walks to first base. 'Now, that's the way to play ball,' young Pete was told. And so he also ran out his walks to first base.

An uncle, Curly Smart, was a clubhouse helper for the Reds. He helped Pete into an extra uniform. While still in high school, Rose was a familiar figure around the team, playing catch with Johnny Temple or Roy McMillan. Another uncle, Buddy Bloebaum, signed Pete. After three years in the minors, he was called up to the big club for spring training of 1963.

Don Blasingame was the Reds' second baseman at the time, a popular teammate. Near the close of camp, Earl Lawson of the *Cincinnati Post* polled the entire squad on what might be the opening-day line-up. Everyone pencilled in Blasingame at second, except Blasingame. He wrote 'Rose'.

'I had been playing enough to think I might have made the team,' Rose said, 'but I still had a minor-league contract when we came home the day before the season opened. Hutch [manager Fred Hutchinson] told me to go get a hotel room that night, and I wondered what he meant. Then he mentioned that he didn't want a lot of my neighbours bothering me. I was starting.'

In his first at-bat against the Pirates' Earl Francis, Rose walked on four pitches and ran to first base. ('What Francis didn't realise was, I couldn't have swung at any of them.') It was the first of 1,566 walks, all of them run out. After Frank Robinson followed with a homer, Rose scored the first of 2,165 runs. A couple of days later, he tripled off Bob Friend for his first of 135 triples, 1,041 extra base hits and 4,256 hits in all, more than anyone else who ever lived.

The other Reds players – actually, the white players – didn't care for Rose. First of all, he had dislodged their buddy, Blasingame. Furthermore, he was coarse and unpresentable, even by baseball's low standards. He had brush-cut hair that, before he was done, would blow to bangs and billow to bouffant. His body was a gunnysack full of cannonballs. He had a gap-toothed grin and was given to flinging himself flat and breaststroking like a gopher into bases.

'That's the best way to get your picture in the morning paper,' he said jauntily, clamping one nostril shut with an index finger and blowing the contents of the other into the grass.

On his first big-league road trip, Rose came in at curfew to find that his reluctant roommate, pitcher Jim Coates, had put the chain on the door. No amount of pleading or pounding moved Coates. 'I didn't know where to go,' Pete said. Remembering that Robinson had missed the trip with injury, Rose knocked on Vada Pinson's door. 'Vada let me stay over. He bought breakfast the next morning. That was the first time I ever had room service. It was twelve dollars and seventy-five cents.' Only Rose remembers the first time he ever had room service. Only Rose remembers how much it was. Only Rose, late in his career, could gaze across a diamond and see knuckleball pitcher Phil Niekro jogging in the outfield, and mutter, 'I got 71 hits off Phil Niekro. I got 41 hits off Joe Niekro. Damn, I wish Mrs Niekro had had another son.'

Rose spent so much time with Pinson and Robinson that Hutchinson began to worry. The following year, during his epic war with cancer, Hutch would be canonised a saint. But he wasn't a saint. 'I'm afraid,' he confided to Earl Lawson of the *Post*, 'Pete is turning nigger on us.'

'The black players were the only ones who treated me like a human being,' Rose told me years later. 'I think now maybe they were able to see something in me.' Robinson put it this way: 'We accepted him for what he was. They called him a hot dog for trying to do things he couldn't. We admired him for labouring beyond his skills. They resented him for taking one of their friends' jobs. Well, we could all relate to that. Nobody had to show him how to hit, but they wouldn't even show him how to be a major-leaguer. So we did.' Rose was the National League's Rookie of the Year. His sophomore season, the Reds lost the pennant on the last day, but the gradual loss of Hutchinson was more traumatic. Rose looked at Hutch and saw his father. 'We watched him go from 220 pounds to 140,' Rose said. 'It was like a skeleton walking into the clubhouse to conduct a meeting, but that skeleton was in charge. This did something to me. It lifted my intensity a level, made me approach long-term goals like they were short-term goals. It made everything urgent.' That off-season, Rose played winter ball in Venezuela for Reggie Otero, Hutch's third-base coach. They were bobbling along on a dilapidated bus, listening to the news on the Spanish radio, when Rose thought he heard the word 'Hutchinson'.

'Reggie started crying,' Rose said. 'I knew Hutch was dead.' The following season was the first of the 15 years that Rose hit .300 or better, the first of his record ten seasons with two hundred hits or more. 'For being Rookie of the Year, I got a $5,000 raise that brought me up to $12,500,' he said. 'I led the league in hits for that. I never dreamed I'd eventually make $10,000 a game.'

Inevitably, most of his dreams were set in the past. 'Throwback' didn't really tell it. It wasn't just that he played like an old-timer, it was as if somehow he had overshot his true generation and become lost in the wrong era. Whenever the umpires signalled a rain delay, Rose raced like a child to the clubhouse radio to hear the old Yankee pitcher Waite Hoyt, the Reds' colour man and Pete's personal Merlin, fill the time with memories. Having been a pallbearer for Babe Ruth, Hoyt was a certified carrier of legends. Near the end of Ruth's life, Hoyt and his wife were leaving the Babe's apartment for the last time when what little was left of Ruth said in that gravelly voice, 'Wait a minute,' and painstakingly got up and went into the kitchen. From the refrigerator he plucked an orchid in a small vase and brought it to Mrs Hoyt. 'Here,' he said, 'I never gave you anything.'

Pete Rose was born in 1941, or as he is more likely to tell you, 'the year of Joe DiMaggio's 56-game hitting streak'. Yet he relayed Hoyt's memories of the 1920s and '30s as if he had been there. 'First of all,' Rose stated authoritatively, 'Ruth always wore the same white terry-cloth bathrobe with a red "B.R." on it' – Pete fastidiously traced the monogram over his left breast – 'and, another thing, he was no lush, like you hear, only beer, bathtubs full of beer . . .'

Re-telling tales of Ty Cobb, Rose animatedly acted them out, clapping the dirt off his thighs just so, snatching up particles of outfield grass in the pristine signal player-manager Cobb had for ordering a knockdown pitch. On the night of his 2,000th hit, Rose mused to almost no notice, 'You know, Cobb took this long to get 1,861.' When games were occasionally lost in labour disputes, Rose fretted, 'Cobb is getting further away.'

That's how long he resided with 4,191.

'How much do you really know about Cobb?' Dave Anderson of the *New York Times* asked Rose as the unreachable record was coming into view. Dave and I were Bob-and-Raying Pete at the Shea Stadium batting cage.

'I know everything about him,' Rose answered typically, 'but the size of his cock.'

In his column the following morning, Anderson discreetly wrote, 'the size of his hat'.

'Did you read Anderson today?' Rose asked me at the ballpark that afternoon.

'Sure.'

'What the fuck was that all about?'

'What do you mean?'

'Seven and five fucking eighths! Seven and five fucking eighths!' This was the ugly way he spoke, even in jest. There was also a pretty way he spoke.

I first met Rose after a 'businessman's special' in Cincinnati, a morning loss that was over so quickly that he was back on the field by early afternoon, in the batting cage. An old coach, George Scherger (Sparky Anderson's original minor-league manager, known to all as 'Sugar Bear'), was throwing batting practice. Children were racing around in the outfield, retrieving the balls in plastic buckets. The only other player left in the ballpark was a young outfielder who had just been told to report to the Triple-A team in Indianapolis and didn't want to take off his Reds uniform just yet. His name was George Foster. He leaned against the back of the cage and silently studied Rose in his kneesprung crouch lasciviously lashing line drive after line drive until Scherger was bent over at the waist, holding his spectacles, puffing.

'Sugar Bear!' Rose called out to the mound, 'I could hit on Christmas morning!'

Turning to Foster, Rose enquired, 'Do you want to hit some?'

'If you got 'em,' Foster said in a whisper.

'If you want 'em, I got 'em all day.'

Capless and stripped to the waist, Rose relieved Scherger and began to pitch.

It took Foster a full bucket to relax. Then the flights to left field smoothed out. The balls started accelerating in mid-air. 'Here comes my curve,' Rose warned. He did have kind of a curve. Foster laughed for the first time. The balls began leaving the park.

'You'll be back,' Rose said softly.

Foster returned to the big leagues to pinch-run in the last game of the play-offs and, on a wild pitch, scored the run that won the pennant. Eventually, Rose would move to third base to make room for Foster in left field (just as he had moved to left field to make room for Tommy Helms at second base, just as he would eventually move to first base to make room for himself on third baseman Mike Schmidt's Philadelphia Phillies). Foster ultimately would have a 52-home-run, 149-RBI season and be named the Most Valuable Player in the National League.

During relentless pennant races with the Dodgers, I always knew where to find Rose if I needed a quote late at night. Even after a doubleheader, he would be sitting in the car in the driveway of his home listening to the LA game on the radio. That was the only receiver he had that could bring in Vin

Scully. A man this one-dimensional should have seemed sadder. His first wife, Karolyn, said, 'There never was a single morning when I didn't see Pete at the kitchen table figuring out his records and averages. What makes him a great success as a ballplayer was what made him fail, in my opinion, in our marriage. He never grew up.'

Pete and Karolyn's son, Petey, haunted the Reds clubhouse in a miniature uniform. At the age of three, Petey took batting practice from Ted Kluszewski, the Bunyanesque hitting coach. Klu flipped rolled-up sweatsocks to the little boy, No. 14, who brandished his toy bat and growled, 'Hey, get this shit over. The fish ain't bitin' today.' Petey would grow up to be a perpetual minor-leaguer who would have just a cup of coffee and a base hit in Cincinnati. Meanwhile, the shy, wide-eyed 'Junior' at Ken Griffey's locker would grow up to be the best player in the game.

Rose's love of baseball could be called his saving grace except, of course, that it didn't save him. It was his grace, anyway. 'Baseball is just about the best thing this country has going for it,' he told me once without embarrassment. 'We're all old ballplayers, aren't we? Who doesn't play baseball? How many girls play football? Is there anything better in the world than the World Series?'

Throughout the 1975 World Series, Rose's most famous one against Boston, he kept asking people if they realised how good it was. Famously, he asked Red Sox catcher Carlton Fisk at home plate and Boston runner Bernie Carbo as Carbo rounded third. While rainstorms stretched out that Series and made it last, Rose was beside himself with wonder. 'I gotta meet Tom Yawkey, too,' he said of the fabled Red Sox owner. 'Christ, I gotta meet Yawkey.'

On one of those rainy days, in a quiet tableau, the Reds went in uniform to exercise at Tufts Fieldhouse, where a turned-over lacrosse goal served as batting practice pitcher Joe

Nuxhall's protective screen. The bus got lost. In full uniform, with cleats clinking and both fists dug into the pockets of his Reds jacket, manager Anderson went into a gas station in the rain to ask directions. The expression on the attendant's face has never gone away. Meanwhile, Rose pumped a guy at the pump on whether he was aware that all of the games but the first were one-run games.

Cincinnati won the Series in seven games, six of them one-run games. Rose was named the Most Valuable Player. Among the Fenway disappointed was a bearded academic wearing a Red Sox cap and pounding a Bobby Doerr mitt, A. Bartlett Giamatti.

The year 1975 also saw catcher Johnny Bench's first marriage, to a New York model named Vickie Chesser. It was the perfectly concise baseball marriage in that it lasted exactly one season. The day after the wedding, they left for spring training. And, immediately following the seventh game with the Red Sox (according to Vickie), John told her, 'Now I'm through with two things I hate: baseball and you.'

'Well, I know he doesn't really hate baseball,' I tried to console her. I first met Vickie beside a baggage carousel on a trip to an All-Star Game. She came up to me and introduced herself.

'Why did you write all that junk about our wedding?' she asked. 'I'm sorry, Vickie,' I said. 'I'm sure I was wrong. I guess you just don't get that many chances to rip a wedding.'

I didn't really rip it. I described it, mentioning that John had invited a lot of popular singers and Hollywood actors (not to mention the President of the United States) but that the biggest celebrity in attendance was ex-Royal Connie Dierking (6 ft 10 in.).

When the Benches 'agreed to disagree', the press release quoted Ernest Borgnine and Ethel Merman invoking that weary phrase, proving that neither Johnny nor Vickie (nor anyone else under the age of 70) had anything to do with the press release.

In Florida the following spring, Bench called and asked me to drop by his hotel room. There was something he wanted to show me, away from the ballpark. He and I weren't bobos, by the way. Far from it.

'What do you make of this?' he asked, handing me a 'notes' column by Dick Young of the *New York Daily News*. Amid a series of dot-dot-dots, Young wrote, 'The reason going around for the Johnny Bench split, I'll never believe in a million years.' Dot-dot-dot.

'It sounds like homosexuality to me,' I said.

'I'm going to kill him.'

'Well, if you do that, it'll be a lot bigger story. As it is, it's pretty innocuous. Why don't you just pull him aside and have it out?' Wanting to write something myself – after all, Cincinnati had treated the union as though it were The Catcher and Mrs Simpson – I asked Bench if we could talk about it.

'No.'

'Just in general terms.'

'I don't want to be quoted,' he said.

'OK,' I told him. 'Just tell me what you can and I won't quote you directly.'

He leaned back on the bed and, after a thoughtful pause, said, 'Don't ever fail if you're Johnny Bench.'

'Time out,' I said. 'Let me use just that one quote.'

He said OK.

So I wrote the 'Don't ever fail if you're Johnny Bench' column, which prompted Vickie to tell me her side of the story. One of her most minor complaints led to a national misunderstanding. Vickie said John brought several friends home on their wedding night to play 'Pong'. Pong was a primitive back-and-forth precursor to today's jazzier electronic games. Evidently, the Associated Press had never heard of it, because the AP changed Pong to Ping-Pong and then sent the story out on the wire.

Besides being the best catcher I ever saw, Bench momentarily became the most dedicated Ping-Pong player of all time.

In his memoirs, *Catch You Later*, Bench implied that Vickie and I were lovers, which, alas, wasn't true. I will admit that I held her once while she cried. 'I had a dream that I punched Callahan out and went to jail for it,' he wrote. (Or his collaborator did, I guess.) The next time I saw John – we were thrown together at a Super Bowl golf tournament – I said, 'You know, you ought to try dreaming of Ingrid Bergman at the top of her game.' By the end of the round, tensions had eased to a point where he could ask, 'Would you tell me something? Why does Hertzel [Cincinnati baseball writer Bob Hertzel] write about Rose every day?'

'Because he has something to say every day,' I said, 'and he says it quickly, while you're still in the trainer's room. Bob's in a hurry. It's 11 o'clock at night. He's on deadline.'

That wasn't the entire story, though. To writers, Pete *was* kind of a narcotic.

Although he neither drank nor smoked, Rose had all of the other old-timers' vices in spades. (Also, diamonds, clubs and hearts.)

'Is it going to rain?' he asked me one nondescript afternoon in the middle of a season.

'Do I look like a meteorologist?' I answered with my customary charm.

'I just don't want to take my "greenie" if we're not going to play,' he said, rolling the pill (a "brownie", as a matter of fact) around in his fist. 'I don't want to be up all night for nothin'.'

For all his vulgarities, Rose had a bright, streety intelligence and was often a pleasure to be around. At the Stage Delicatessen in New York City, he summoned the maitre d' to complain that there was no Pete Rose sandwich. 'Reggie Jackson . . . Tom Seaver . . . Susan Anton. What kind of fucking year has Susan Anton had?' And Rose was practically the only man in sports who rotated his similes.

'Forbes Field?' he exclaimed one year, recalling the old home of the Pittsburgh Pirates. 'Forbes Field was as hard as Chinese arithmetic!' 'Forbes Field?' he shouted in a different context the following year. 'Forbes Field was as hard as a hundred dollars' worth of jawbreakers!' A man who rotates his similes can be awfully hard to resist.

Rose was arrogant to big shots (I stood in the Oval Office with him once when he was barely civil to Jimmy Carter) but the clubhouse men loved Pete. He browbeat the sapphire salesmen into cutting the trainers and roustabouts in on the All-Star rings. When Earl Lawson of the *Post* retired, Rose, not Lawson's paper, quietly bought him the gold watch of sweet and corny tradition. Pete could be rough, but he wasn't mean. He was a primitive, but he wasn't a bully.

'If you'd have been here last week,' he told me at a batting cage, 'I'd have kicked your ass.'

'Here I am right now,' I replied, being Irish.

'If I thought you'd fight back, I would.'

'Put that worry out of your mind,' I said. 'I always fight back.' He ran full-speed to the outfield wall and returned at a trot with his callused hand extended.

'I suppose you're aware,' said the Dayton writer Si Burick, 'that you'd have to kill him to stop him.'

Rose's obsessions seemed so charming then. Moving over to Philadelphia, just to show the Phillies how to win a world championship, he glowed like a filament in Clearwater, Florida.

'Have you seen the schedule?' he whispered.

'No,' I said.

'We open in Minnesota.'

'I thought Minnesota was in the American League.'

'It's an exhibition game, but it's the first game in the Hubert Humphrey Dome. Get it?'

'Get what?'

'We're the visitors!'

'So?'

'I'm leading off! I got a chance to get the first hit in the Humphrey Fucking Dumphrey Dome!'

Rose always preferred the road to home because there was always a ninth inning on the road.

Quite a long time later, I suddenly thought to ask him, 'Whatever happened to the first hit in the Humphrey Dumphrey Dome?'

'It's rolling around in my dresser drawer right now,' he said. I thought of this much later when the papers were saying he was having to sell his memorabilia.

Of the Baseball Annies, Rose partook lavishly, Homerically, until a Tampa woman became pregnant, thereby ending Pete's 16-year marriage to Karolyn. 'Watch him go now,' whispered second baseman Joe Morgan, the wisest Reds player. The worse shambles Pete's life was, the greater haven the field was. Rose proceeded to get a hit in 44 straight games.

He wasn't shy about his gambling, either. He quizzed everyone around him on the basketball spreads. Into microphones, he spun animated tales of Chicago speakeasies, as if he had been along with Waite Hoyt's Yankees when, speaking too loudly about 'the Big Guy', they suddenly found themselves in the presence of Al Capone. 'If you wanted an autograph from the Big Guy,' Rose advised seriously, 'you better not go inside your pocket for a pen.' Wistfully, he added, 'Wouldn't you like to have met the Big Guy? He'd have had to give you a tip on a horse or something, wouldn't he?'

But little guys, incredibly little, would do Rose in. Rather, they would help Pete do himself in. Baseball Commissioner

Giamatti and ex–Mob prosecutor John Dowd would regard them as Al Capones.

Unlike Ruth, who, it was said, couldn't be a manager because he couldn't manage himself, Rose, near the finish, was brought back to Cincinnati as a playing-manager to stimulate flagging business. Dropping in salary from $2 million to $500,000 (plus an attendance clause), he applied for and received the Players' Association's permission to take a cut over the maximum 20 per cent. 'Where would I be,' he said with that jack-o'-lantern grin, 'without the Players' Association?'

As a manager, especially when he was also playing, Rose was backstopped by the old coach, Scherger. 'George doesn't tell me what to do,' he said, 'but if he did, I'd do it.' On a baseball field, Rose always knew what to do. But he was better with the younger players than the ones who had prowled with him in the past, and he was best of all with the rookie-league beginners, the instructional-league kids. 'I'm the same as any one of you,' he reminded them sincerely at the close of his orientation lecture, 'who has two arms, two legs and four thousand hits.'

Sitting at the manager's desk, filling out his line-up card (having just asked me how to spell the name of that night's starting Reds pitcher), Rose said, 'I'm not scared to say how much I love the game, but my players are. Maybe it's because everyone knows how much money they make, but today's young players hold something in. Just on the field and in public. It comes out in the clubhouse when only the other players can see.'

One recommendation every old manager makes to every new one is to execute the squad cuts briskly. But Rose couldn't do it. 'If they want to,' he said, 'I'll talk all day.' In the year of the record hit, the last of the spring cuts was a sloe-eyed and red-freckled pitcher named Ron Robinson, nicknamed 'True

Creature' by his sensitive teammates. After an extended monologue and a lengthy silence, Rose asked, 'Is there anything you want to say?'

'Yes,' the pitcher said finally, 'I hope you don't get any more hits.'

'What did you say?'

'I hope you stop hitting.' In a smaller voice, Robinson added, 'Because I don't want you to get the hit until I get back.'

This is the kind of thing that touches the great roughneck. 'Don't worry,' Rose whispered. 'I'll wait for you.' True Creature chalked up his first major-league hit in Cincinnati the night before Rose collected his 4,192nd, a single. Pete's ovation went on for many minutes. As he stood on first base and thought of his father, he felt completely alone. For the first time on a baseball field, he didn't know what to do. Like a child frightened by the noise, he started to cry. Petey, who was now taller than Pete, ran out of the dugout wearing his own No. 14 uniform. They stood there in an embrace for several minutes. Pete dropped his head on his son's shoulder. 'It was the first time he ever hugged me,' Petey said. 'But we've never seen each other since then when we haven't hugged.'

Later in that historic game, Rose tripled into the left-field corner, exactly as he had against Bob Friend 22 years earlier. For just an instant, Pete appeared to be starting over. After the game, Rose didn't compare himself to Cobb except to say, 'I don't steal bases like he did, and he didn't wear a tie on the road like I do.'

In the final three games that Rose started, he went 8 for 13 at the plate, including his tenth five-for-five game, one of thirteen records he set that day alone. However, in what would turn out to be his last at-bat in the major leagues (he wouldn't confirm it was his last for over a year), he struck out on three Goose Gossage fastballs. 'I had two strikes on me,' he told me later, 'before I could get the fucking doughnut off the bat.'

When he finally declared himself a full-time manager, he said, 'It wouldn't be fair for me to say I'm going to miss hitting the ball, because I got to hit it more than anybody. To my knowledge, there's never been an athlete who performed before as many people as I have. Twenty-four seasons, seventeen All-Star Games, eight play-offs, six World Series.

'People wonder why I didn't pinch-hit myself last season for a ceremonial goodbye, but a manager can't play a guy unless that particular guy is supposed to be playing that particular game, that particular inning, that particular situation.'

Let the situation ethicists take a ride on that.

As Rose played less and less, probably he gambled more and more. Maybe he had to put himself on the line in some riskier fashion than just pencil-marking line-up cards.

Nobody doubted Rose sent surrogates to the racetrack windows to foil the IRS. Nobody doubted he took cash at trading card shows so he wouldn't have to declare it. He was still denying the critical count in 2003 (though not for much longer), but few doubted that Rose bet on baseball through those incredibly seedy Cincinnati musclemen who tossed him over to soften their own minor-league drug and firearm raps. On the evidence of telephone records, bank receipts and betting slips (in Pete's handwriting, experts alleged), baseball claimed to have documented 412 wagers between April and July of 1987, including 52 on the Reds to win. Since 1919, when the Reds were the beneficiaries of the Chicago Black Sox scandal, betting on baseball has been the sport's ultimate crime, although betting against yourself, not to mention ensuring the bet, would seem to be the mortal sin. Nobody suggested Rose did that. Nobody who knew Rose could imagine it. John Dowd didn't know Rose.

In October of 1990, while Pete was serving his five-month prison sentence for tax evasion, the team he put together upset the Oakland A's in a World Series sweep. Manager Lou Piniella took the bows.

After the fourth game in Oakland, as the champagne was flying ('For barbarians like that,' Red Smith used to say, 'Dr Pepper is too good'), Reds coach Tony Perez sat in a corner of a cramped office, sipping the wine slowly. In the glory days of the Big Red Machine, the big Cuban was just as indispensable as Rose, Morgan or Bench. Tony's hatred of the Latin stereotype was such that he refused to let Davey Concepcion, Cesar Geronimo or anyone else contribute to it. Despite some 1,650 RBI, Perez was made to wait for an unseemly while in the Hall of Fame vestibule but finally entered with Sparky Anderson and Boston catcher Carlton Fisk in 2000 (all featured actors in the '75 Series). 'What do you think Pete's doing right now?' I asked Tony. 'Cheering,' he said. It had been in the paper that the warden at Marion Prison in Illinois had extended the evening hours so the inmates could watch the World Series at a community TV set. Rose probably sat near the front, helping deliver the play-by-play.

'What do you think he had on the game?' Perez asked me.

'I don't know,' I said. 'In the movies it's always cigarettes.' Tony laughed and sighed at the same time. 'Pete has all the cigarettes tonight,' he said, 'and he doesn't even smoke.'

After Rose's release, I went to West Palm Beach, Florida, to visit Pete in exile, to play golf with him. I had resolved not to open the conversation with jail but he did just that. 'I was the best tennis player in prison,' he said even before we finished shaking hands. 'I was the second-best horseshoe-thrower.' Years before, he had learned tennis in a blitz for an *ABC's Superstars* competition, finishing second in the tennis segment of that TV decathlon to Columbia and Lakers basketball star Jim McMillian. (In a swimming segment, boxer Joe Frazier damned near drowned.) Now, hitting right-handed off his back leg, Pete was learning golf.

With a twinkle, he said, 'They wouldn't let us play a whole lot of golf in prison. But you could play tennis – doubles – as long as your team was able to hold the court. A fellow named Larry Brodi and I held it every day from 3.30 p.m. till just before the eight o'clock count. My knees ached so bad, I had to roll out of bed in the morning.'

His second wife, a second Carol (a former barmaid and Philadelphia Eagles cheerleader), had come with him to the golf course in a two-Porsche caravan. Not all of the money was gone. She had their six-year-old son, Ty, in tow. Pete had lobbied for Tyrus but settled for Tyler.

'If I had been chasing Schmedley Milton all those years,' Rose said, 'I would never have named my kid "Schmedley". But Ty Rose, there's a name for you.' Ty was already driving himself to first grade in a golf cart. 'That's got to be a record,' Rose said, 'doesn't it?'

He had brought me a golf shirt emblazoned 'Hit King' over the left breast, like 'B.R.' on a white terry-cloth bathrobe. 'Here,' Rose said. 'I never gave you anything.'

Pete could be kept out of baseball but not out of the public prints. In one of the many interviews that Rose never stopped giving, Jane Pauley asked him if he'd like someday to be the subject of a movie. She may have been startled by how cleanly he fielded the question and how quickly he threw it home. 'Yes, because movies usually have happy endings,' he said, 'and that would mean I made it to the Hall of Fame.'

In 1999, corporate sponsorships cornered baseball into inviting Rose to the World Series to stand alongside Willie Mays, Ted Williams and Hank Aaron as one of the players elected by the fans to an All-Century Team. In the midst of their retirement, Mays and Mickey Mantle had been excused from old-timers games briefly for shilling at Bally's Park Place and Del Webb's Claridge Casino Hotel in Atlantic City. When baseball loosened its policy against golfing and schmoozing with known gamblers, Mays and Mantle were reinstated. The Mick expressed his relief interestingly. 'You don't want to get thrown out of your favourite bar,' he said.

The All-Century Team also included Brooks Robinson, who, along with football's Johnny Unitas, basketball's Walt Frazier and hockey's Phil Esposito, once donned a tuxedo to dance around in a craps-game commercial, like so many Sky Mastersons in a velveteen sewer, shaking imaginary dice and warbling 'Bal-ly's, Bal-ly's'.

Although the World Series was in Atlanta, the biggest ovation during the All-Century Team ceremony was not for Aaron but for Rose. One had wondered if there'd be boos or begrudged applause. There was an explosion of cheers. 'I just think they've missed him,' Joe Morgan said in the broadcast booth.

Morgan had been adamant that Pete must own up and apologise before any return. 'I've missed him,' Joe said. In a sideline interview, NBC's Jim Gray made like a prosecutor, trawling for a confession. The fans sided with Rose.

Dowd, the real prosecutor, worried that Jean Valjean was getting away. First quietly, then politely, finally impolitely, indignantly, baseball asked Dowd to shut up. He took this as a signal that reinstatement was thinkable.

'Somebody has to stand up for Bart,' he said.

A. Bartlett Giamatti was a Renaissance man at Yale but a romantic at baseball. Like Rose, he had started out as a second baseman. But Giamatti failed to make his high school team in South Hadley, Massachusetts, and ended up the equipment manager. Just eight days after the ordeal of banning Rose, Commissioner Giamatti dropped dead at 51, mostly from cigarettes. But his friend and successor, Fay Vincent, considered Rose an accomplice. Vincent and Dowd were classmates at the Yale Law School. The whole thing became personal. Vincent was not a long-standing baseball man, though unknown to Pete and most people, he truly did have a deep feeling for the game. To Rose, Vincent was just a money man whose college sport had been football until a dormitory prank left him permanently on a cane. Giamatti was disgusted to hear a report that Rose referred to Vincent as 'the cripple'. It certainly sounds like Pete. Rose may hate Vincent and Dowd. The funny thing is, Pete liked, and still likes, Giamatti. Maybe it's not so funny. Giamatti loved baseball. In 2002, at the World Series in San Francisco, Rose again walked onto the field to an amazing ovation. This time he upstaged Baltimore Orioles Ironman Cal Ripken, whose eclipse of Lou Gehrig topped a cock-eyed list of the sport's Most Memorable Moments. While Rose's record hit was an appropriate also-ran in the voting, Pete finished first on the applause meter.

Commissioner Bud Selig started to look into how he could let Rose into the Hall of Fame and yet keep him out of baseball. The trouble with this was, Pete wanted a place in the game – a job, an income – even more than a pedestal at Cooperstown (though he coveted that terribly).

'Do you think I'll ever get in?' Rose asked me on the golf course.

'No,' I said.

'How can you say that?' he whispered.

I wished I hadn't been so blunt. 'Pete, why don't you just declare, "That's a nice little Hall of Fame they have up there in Cooperstown. It's got the guy with the second-most hits in it." Wouldn't that be more like you?'

He shook his head.

The many people Rose now appalls surely must realise that a higher form of man may not have had all those hits. Babe Ruth, who liked to urinate on his teammates in the shower, didn't grow up to be David Niven, either.

Early in 2004, in a crass media blitz and a clueless book (*My Prison Without Bars*), Rose at last confessed to betting on the team he managed. I liked the title of his book. When she was still married to Pete, Karolyn told me, 'Someday you and I will write a book together. We'll call it, *Wife of the Switch-Hitter* or *Are You Sure This Is the Way to Cooperstown?*'

For many Julys, whenever a new Hall of Fame class was inducted, baseball's banished star had come to upstate New York anyway, setting up shop at a Main Street storefront, 'Pete Rose's Collectibles,' signing autographs for money. 'Pete Rose . . . Pete Rose . . . Pete Rose . . . Pete Rose . .' He could write his name faster than just about any man who ever lived.

But in 2003, when Eddie Murray and Gary Carter were stuffed and mounted, Rose had diplomatically stayed away. Some kind of parole, maybe not a full pardon, was rumoured to be in the works, and Pete was hopeful enough to lie low for once. Whitey Ford and Yogi Berra took his place in the autograph shop.

'Whitey likes to sign 'em "Ed Ford",' Rose told me years ago, 'because it's only six letters. The Pope has him beat, though. "J P II." You know, when I heard a Polish Cardinal had been named Pope, I thought it was Stan Musial.'

An hour before a night World Series game in wintry Shea Stadium, the wind was whistling and everyone was bundled up in overcoats and mufflers, including Roy Campanella. Roxy, his wife, expertly backed Campanella's wheelchair into the press box elevator. As the door shut, a sheaf of newspaper blew in behind them.

'Campy's Hit in 11th Wins Game Three,' read the headline.

For just a second, the three people on the elevator forgot there was a Bert Campaneris.

'Campy,' I muttered when I came to.

'I know,' he said.

8

Sweet and Neglected Games

At the Winter Games of Lake Placid, a prefabricated wooden way station called the Austria House served as a lifesaver to journalists. Wine and beer flowed. Music oompahed. And the thirstier reporters huddled there into the night to try to forget a bus system that was driving a lot of people to drink but no one to Saranac Lake.

A few days before the Games opened, on an especially frosty evening, a normally circumspect American mistook Annemarie Moser-Proell for a hostess and asked the skiing goddess to dance. It was an understandable faux pas. She was wearing the puffy peasant dress that all of Austria's women athletes would wear in the opening ceremonies. But, as approachable as she looked in crinoline, Ms Moser-Proell took the invitation badly. A row ensued.

Just as fur and furniture were ready to fly, the Yank was yanked out of the maelstrom by a strong-gripped but soft-spoken downhill racer named Leonhard, who described himself as Austria's fourth-string downhiller. It wasn't even a sure thing that Leonhard would be allowed to race. He may have come all of this way just to stand at the bottom of the mountain and clap for defending champion Franz Klammer.

'The downhill is baseball to an Austrian,' Leonhard explained when peace was restored and the music resumed. 'Except much bigger. It's everything to me.' A few days later, to the astonishment of the Austrians and everyone else, Leonhard Stock won the Olympic downhill, the World Series. Klammer was the one who stood at the bottom of the mountain and clapped.

At the Austria House later, Leonhard took the gold medal out of his pocket and rubbed it briskly on the arm of the American.

'You know,' he said, 'I think Annemarie will dance with us now.'

JOY ENTERS THE HOUSE

Great Britain's Daley Thompson, the natural heir to Jim Thorpe, was only 18 when the Summer Games came to Montreal in 1976. Watching Bruce Jenner's triumph from the shadow of 18th place, the youngest decathlete made a wish: not just to win the Olympic gold medal but to win it three times. Even before his 1980 victory in Moscow, Thompson declared himself in writing. 'I got a postcard from Russia,' recalled the only two-time champion (1948 and '52), Bob Mathias. 'All it said was: "I'm going for three."'

At Los Angeles in 1984, Thompson was a loud and wonderful cinch. Mathias had to move over. Carl Lewis had to get out of the way. The world had a new greatest athlete.

Thorpe won his Olympic decathlon at Stockholm in 1912. 'You, sir,' declared King Gustav, 'are the world's greatest athlete.' To which Thorpe replied with touching simplicity, 'Thanks, King.' Thompson didn't complain about the title (he didn't object to any praise), but he told me in London, 'It's just a tag, really. It's true that we're all Thorpe's descendants, though – Mathias, Rafer Johnson, Jenner, me. We've shared something. It's passed down from one to the next. It's never anyone's property. It's only mine for the moment.'

The moment was running out; that's why I had come to see him.

His square name is Francis Morgan Thompson. 'Daley' is a corruption of Ayodele, an African endearment bestowed by his Nigerian father and mispronounced by his Scottish mother. It means 'joy enters the house'. ('That was the only thing,' in Thompson's bittersweet estimation, 'that they got absolutely right.') His London childhood was something out of Thackeray, not Dickens, though classic shadows like boarding schools were included. 'Since forever, I always thought I was going to be the best in the world at something. My school friends used to laugh at me, but I kept searching for the thing that would express who I am. There's only one key for every lock, you know. As soon as I found the decathlon, I knew it was me.'

Though at first he resisted the idea of giving up sprinting, the perverseness of specialising in versatility appealed to his sense of justice and mischief. 'In any walk of life, there'll always be a bloke more talented in this or that, who's smarter in some way, or richer, or faster, or just better suited. But can the thing that he was given be lined up against everything you've got?' At just over 6 ft, 195 pounds, much too thick and blocky for the pole-vaulting and long-distance running, though not nearly brawny enough for the shot-putting and spear-throwing, Thompson was ideally constructed for none of the ten disciplines. 'But I'm happy with my dimensions,' he said. 'I've got by so far. Would I change anything at all? Sure, I would. I'd take Paul Newman's eyes.'

The Olympics stirred Thompson. 'As a concept,' he said, 'I think it's one of the most genuinely humanitarian thoughts that man has ever had. The youth of the world coming together to play – it's a wonderful dream, isn't it?' He regularly skipped the opening parade to save his legs from the speeches and his head from the pigeons, but he always participated in the casual camaraderie around the Olympic Village. 'I'm a Village person,' he said. 'I like to go about and meet gymnasts and weightlifters, every kind of athlete. We share a special understanding. All sports are the same; it's only the rules that are different. Were Michael Jordan and I to meet, I honestly think we could communicate without sentences, with just the start of words, maybe with knowing nods alone. At the Olympics, I love watching almost anything at all that's special, as long as it doesn't have a horse in it.'

For someone who was pulling down hundreds of thousands sipping soft drinks on billboards, Thompson sounded remarkably like an amateur. 'I like to think of myself as one of the last true amateurs,' he said, 'but I can only be an amateur because I can afford to be. Inside, though, that's exactly what I am. I love the occasion and I can't help showing it. At the end of the day, I think that's the real reason why the public doesn't enjoy Carl Lewis. He never looks to be having a good time.'

Thompson often trained in California. As he said, 'It can be nice to get away from the English ambience. If you're at all aggressive – gung ho – it's really kind of frowned upon here. Whereas, in America, they appreciate that. In fact, it's a prerequisite to getting around. For everybody on the street, every day is a competition.' Not all American traits pleased him, of course, and one was especially troubling. 'People in the US tend to value a sport or a sportsman exactly according to how much money is involved. In adjacent arenas, if Carl Lewis and Ben Johnson were running for a $1,000 prize, and six monkeys were racing for $10 million, which place do you think would be filled? Honestly, if Jesse Owens and Jim Thorpe were around today, I wonder if as many people would have heard of them.'

On practice fields at UCLA or the University of California at Irvine, he occasionally encountered the heptathlete Jackie Joyner-Kersee. 'A very pleasant girl,' he said, 'and a beautiful athlete.' (She told me that at every encounter Thompson would brush her with a dare or nudge her with an insult. 'He was the one who challenged me to go over 7,000 points in the heptathlon. "Why not be the first?" he said. Or he'd go the other way: "Nobody will ever jump 24 feet in the heptathlon. Give me a break!" I knew exactly what he was doing. He was showing me how to be the absolute best. He had been the absolute best for so very long.')

But Daley's unbeaten summers ended abruptly at nine, one year before Seoul. Torsten Voss, an East German built like an East German, pushed past him. So did the West German, 6 ft 7 in. tall Jurgen Hingsen, Thompson's historic foil. Still, Daley pressed on. In the world championships leading up to the 1988 Games, he finished a poignant ninth. Thompson began to enter only fragments of events, with desultory results. 'I'm going for three,' he had written.

'I have an inordinate amount of faith in my own ability to do things,' he said crisply, though his voice and manner had softened since 1984. The charming braggadocio that had run to self-aggrandising T-shirts was muted considerably. Yet, when asked how he was, he still replied, 'A little short of fantastic.' Marriage had settled Thompson, too, and the birth of a daughter 12 weeks prematurely had jumbled his regimen. 'My little girl weighed less than a bag of sugar. It was incredible how tiny she was. Yet she was perfectly formed.'

What kept him competing?

'I haven't finished justifying all the work I've put in,' he said. 'I don't think of it as the work since the last success but as the work since the very beginning. To me, it's always been accumulative.'

But wasn't Korea a long way to go to lose?

'No matter how it has gone or how it goes,' he said, 'I wouldn't change anything. It fulfils me to be what I am. Even to lose. Yes, I'll be there, even to lose.'

And so Daley Thompson never made it to three. All the same, he got to where he was going. He considered the wish fulfilled.

'Because I've learned it isn't the medals,' he said. 'The medals don't mean anything. And it isn't the glory. The glory doesn't last. It's performing well, and more than that, feeling deeply about it.'

Thanks, King.

DISONISCHENKO

For Montreal's Summer Games, some of the press were billeted in dormitories at the University of Montreal, two buses and a subway from anywhere. Sally Quinn of the *Washington Post* was with us there for about five minutes, but seeing Detroit columnist Joe Falls in the hallway in his underwear, she moved into a Holiday Inn. Over the entire fortnight, only one event was staged at the university, and the saddest story of the Games involved a southern sportswriter who looked at the schedule that morning and refused to saddle up.

'There's something here, and I'm covering whatever's here,' he said stubbornly. What was there was fencing, and not even the fencing proper, just the fencing segment of the Modern Pentathlon. That was George S. Patton's Olympic event, a pantomime of a soldier fighting his way back from behind enemy lines: running, riding, swimming, fencing, shooting.

Later that day, word drifted to the more popular venues that the Soviet pentathlete and defending gold medalist Boris Onischenko (immediately renamed 'Disonischenko') had been caught with a battery in his nose cone. Pressing a button hidden in his glove, Boris was setting off his own touchés. Our man had a world exclusive.

'You lucky bastard,' we greeted him at the end of the long commute. 'Yeah, it was pretty good,' he said, leaning back in his easy chair.

'What did Onischenko have to say?'

'Onis who?'

TONIGHT

As they originally exercised in the nude, Greek Olympians probably never envisioned Winter Games. But the smaller festivals are the sweeter ones. There's a charm to chilblains. Usually coming straight from the Super Bowl, US sportswriters stand ready with their most penetrating questions, such as: 'Just how tall do you have to be to qualify for the giant slalom?'

Also, the Americans do very little of the winning in the snow, which is a relief to the eardrum. Their ambitions are modest.

'I want to ski through the Norwegian pines again,' sang the US Nordic racer John Aalberg in Lillehammer, 'and maybe beat a few Norwegians.' (He was born in Norway.)

'I want to beat some Norwegians,' a teammate joined in.

'So do I,' said another.

But, at the end of their line, a jug-eared kid of 19, Ryan Heckman, shook his head. 'I want to *meet* some Norwegians,' he said. 'Girls.' With a flash of braces, Heckman winced and admitted, 'I've been smiling so much, I've got cuts all over the inside of my mouth.'

Summer or winter, the Olympics is a great place for meeting girls, even women. It belongs to them, you know.

After his third misbegotten Games, in Albertville, France, speed skater Dan Jansen was asked if he'd be back; and, of course, he would be. Yes, he said, maybe, probably, he hoped so, sure, perhaps, he guessed. Jansen's wife, Robin, stood beside him as he rocked and sputtered in the perfect illustration of the masculine state.

'We have to talk about a lot of things,' Jansen concluded, nodding toward his wife. 'We're going to start a family, I don't know when.'

'Tonight,' she said decisively, and the press conference ended.

A KIND OF GRACE

'I've read and heard that I've been described as an ape,' Jackie Joyner-Kersee said in Seoul, breaking some of the listeners' hearts. 'I never thought I was the prettiest person in the world. But I know that, inside, I'm beautiful.' At a luncheonette in Los Angeles some months before the Games, she and her coach-husband, Bob Kersee, sat with me in a booth and, for once, he let her do most of the talking. She described the porch in East St Louis, Illinois, where she learned to jump. She told me how the sand for her porchside landing pit had been purloined from the nearest recreation centre a scoop at a time in a potato chip bag. She spoke of her parents, Alfred Joyner and Mary Gaines, who were 14 and 16 on the day they wed.

And she defined women's athletics in words, just as she had been doing it in actions.

'I don't think being an athlete is unfeminine,' said Jackie, who was named for a First Lady and now *was* a First Lady. 'I think of it as a kind of grace.'

ANNIE

'Hi, I'm Annie,' said a 25-year-old Chinese Myrna Loy with the Olympic Commission in Beijing.

'Hello,' I answered, 'I'm Lin Phong.'

'Is your name really Lin Phong?'

'Is your name really Annie?'

'I'm Xie Bin,' she said.

'I'm Tom Callahan.'

She was the interpreter for the Commission.

A bureaucrat in a room of teapots and doilies said through Xie, 'The first survey among Chinese people showed 91.6 per cent supported Beijing in its bid for an Olympic Games. In the second, 98.3 per cent supported a bid.' (I didn't say anything, but I thought, 'Here's to the 1.7 per cent in China who still say no to government surveys.')

'What influence,' I asked, 'should the Tiananmen Square massacre have on the Olympics choosing or not choosing Beijing?'

'Since the Tiananmen accident in 1989,' Xie translated the bureaucrat's careful reply, 'different people have different opinions. As time is passing, history itself will answer this problem. At the time, some Western media had exaggerated reports. I have some friends in the United States and France who tell me that when the Tiananmen accident is talked about now, perceptions have already changed. But the Tiananmen accident should be totally separated from Beijing's Olympic ambition.'

'You keep saying "accident",' I said. 'Is this a difficulty of language? Do you mean "incident"? You can't mean "accident".'

Without translating, Xie dropped her head, folded her hands in her lap and said in a whisper, 'It's a difficulty of language.'

For her sake, I changed the subject to the kindness of the people in the street and in the Forbidden City, to their curious eyes and their ready laughter. 'Yes,' she resumed translating with a sigh. 'If you talk to the citizens, they don't talk too much about Tiananmen. What Chinese people are concerned with mostly these days is the economy.'

Walking out with Xie, I surmised, 'In 1989, you must have been a student yourself.'

'I was,' she said, 'an English student.'

'And you didn't know or hear much about Tiananmen?'

'I was too busy worrying about a job.'

We parted at the elevator, but on the ground floor she came rushing out of the stairwell. This time, Xie wanted to speak for herself.

'If it's true,' she said, 'it's sad.' As though this were costing her in some way, she added, 'I think maybe something did happen.' And she wanted to tell me one other thing, about the Western names so many of the Chinese had adopted to do business.

'I took "Kathy" before "Annie",' she said. 'We were permitted to choose for ourselves. But I decided I didn't like "Kathy". What does "Annie" mean, do you know?'

'Yes,' I lied. 'It means "Angel".'

'Then it is a good name?'

'For you, it is.'

NOT FOR THE LOVE OF THE SEA

Two photographers, one from the *New York Times*, were strolling out of the Anaheim Marriott one night when suddenly it hit them. They weren't thinking of anything. What hit them was a Nissan Sentra.

Their legs were broken: all four of them. Tommy Lasorda of the Los Angeles Dodgers, who, like the photographers, was on his way to the Friday night Super Bowl party, knelt down and comforted them.

Under the Nissan, whose driver had mistaken the accelerator for the brake, were a mangled set of golf clubs, a smashed computer and an exploded suitcase, all of which belonged to me. A moment before, they had been sitting under a stone bench that was now scattered in chunks all over the property. Two moments before, I had been sitting on that bench, waiting for an airport limousine. Abruptly, *Time* had decided to put yachtsman Dennis Conner on the cover, and I was discreetly sneaking away to Australia. When the smoke cleared and I reached the airport just in time, a suspicious woman at the airline counter said, 'Most people travelling to Australia have at least one bag.' After a day's flight to Sydney, another long leg to Perth, a race to the dock, a ride on a tender named *Betsy* and a relay on an orange rubber ducky that scooted like a water bug across the waves, I was delivered to *Stars & Stripes* in the middle of the Indian Ocean.

'Are you a sailor?' Conner asked instead of saying hello.

'I know everything there is to know about sailing,' I said, 'except who's this fellow Halyard I keep hearing about?'

He didn't smile. 'Then stand behind me,' he said. 'My men know me so well, I don't even say "I'm coming about" anymore. If this boom hits you, it'll kill you.'

A 132-year winning streak, the longest in all of sports, had been broken over the ample shoulders of this sullen non-swimmer in the back of the boat. ('It's my job to stay out of the water,' he said.) On a winged keel three years earlier, an appealing gang of Australians had flown the America's Cup away to a western backwater called Fremantle. Until then, the America's Cup had seemed to be a boat race in the horse racing sense of the term. The only American who had ever lost the Cup was about to retrieve it.

'I don't like to sail,' said the greatest sailor in the world. 'I guess I don't dislike it. It's just a bottom line to me. I like to compete.' His hands were far from delicate, but their impression on the helm was something like that. 'Feels more like a bull fiddle today,' mused Conner, at whose touch it was usually a violin, a Stradivarius. In a continuous search where a tenth of a knot was considered a quantum find, he was thought to be worth a full knot himself. Conner could read the wind as it rippled on your shirt. To his salt-stung eyes, tiny fractions of speed were visible on the fabrics of the sails that he pinched and reshaped punctiliously.

His lips were smeared with white goo. 'Put some of this on,' he said crossly, being uncomfortable with kindness.

The anonymous sailors of *Stars & Stripes*, well-educated men slaving for $75 a week, believed Conner could see past the horizon. Why he tacked on this wave instead of the last one or the next one was a mystery to all of them, and a thrill.

'Dennis?' a voice came over a squawker from either the trailing *Betsy* or the helicopter whirling overhead. 'Could you ask your guest to duck down for a few minutes so the photographers can take some pictures?' I was the only one on the boat wearing bright yellow slickers.

'OK,' Conner said.

'Stay where you are,' he told me after he signed off. 'Fuck those guys.' I went forward anyway and hid by the grinders until I was as green as the sea. Not on the cover, thankfully, but in the otherwise beautiful opening *Time* spread, a careful eye will detect two long yellow legs sticking out from under the boom.

'Will anybody be heartbroken if we change this sail?' Conner enquired rhetorically. 'Shall we put up Dolly?'

'Dolly' was a revolutionary, not to mention provocative, new spinnaker named for Miss Parton. It featured rows of billowing bulges that plumped out into pouches of wind. 'I love the way she shakes those thingies,' Conner sang. His late father had been a Convair engineer who dabbled in commercial fishing. The way some kids haunted pool halls, Dennis haunted marinas. Had he been born in Indianapolis or Lexington instead of San Diego, he would have haunted garages or stables. In his 40s, he still referred to sailing as 'a good way to hang out'. A junior membership was eventually extended by the San Diego Yacht Club, and the somewhat stout and uncoordinated boy with no real love of the sea began tweaking and fiddling and driving the sport crazy.

'You know how a lot of men say someday they'll go sailing?' Conner asked me, back on land. 'My father never stopped working. I don't know how much vacation time he had accrued at the end, when he died of cancer.'

'But you and your men aren't just going sailing, are you?' I said.

'No.'

'Ted Turner says you've squeezed the fun out of the game.'

'That's just an excuse to lose.'

'So, what do you require from a fellow sailor?'

Conner thought it over for a moment. 'If a crew member will put this ahead of his religion,' he said, 'his family, his girlfriend, his home, his career, then I'll give him a try-out.' When I finished writing the story, it was 7 a.m. Monday morning. John Dunn, the *Time* bureau chief in Australia, came in with coffee. 'Hey, who won that Super Bowl?' I asked.

'It's only Sunday in Anaheim,' Dunn said. 'I was just coming to get you. The Aussies have bought the feed. They've set up in a Quonset hut and we're invited.'

The game was just about to begin.

COVERING A WAR

One year at Indianapolis – the definitive year at Indy – Art Pollard died in practice, Salt Walther was maimed in the first turn, Swede Savage was killed in the fourth turn and an STP crewman named Armondo Teran, who was 22, was run over by a fire truck rushing the wrong way up the pit lane to reach Savage. Teran, who wouldn't have thought to look left as well as right on the all-time one-way street, died, too.

The sound Teran made first on the fender of the truck and then on the pavement of pit row resonated, along with the dainty way famed engine-builder George Bignotti collected Teran's shoes, and the vacant expression on Gordon Johncock's face when the 500 Mile Race was awarded to him after just 332½ miles. Late that night in Gasoline Alley, after the writing, before the drinking, Merle Bettenhausen tried to explain auto racing to an infidel. It's a famous name at Indianapolis, Bettenhausen. Merle's father, Tony, died there in a practice run. 'I'll be right back,' he had said. Merle's brothers, Gary and Tony Jr, raced there without much luck. Merle would have tried the Brickyard as well, but his arm was sliced off in a Michigan 200. There must also have been some fire, because the skin of his face was stretched and shiny pink. Nervously, Merle hinged and unhinged his artificial arm, clicking his hook's pincers like castanets.

'I know why you feel sorry for me,' he said, 'but you don't know why I feel sorry for you. We are discoverers. You may be alive, and you may have two arms. But you have never felt it.'

But I could hear it. In the sobs coming from the closed garages, I could certainly hear it.

GOOD SAVE

Down to one goaltender, awaiting a replacement from the minor leagues, the Oilers recruited an Edmonton policeman, Floyd Whitney, for a practice session. 'You're the target today, eh?' one of the stubbly giants greeted him reassuringly.

Though the pace of the scrimmage seemed as brisk as a regular game's, helmets were discarded and the blush of exhilaration showed on everyone's face but especially on Wayne Gretzky's. Inoffensively, he laughed at the good plays and dropped his long jaw and howled at the mistakes, drawing good-natured curses all around.

Amazingly, just about every Gretzky rifle shot was snared in Officer Whitney's first baseman's mitt. *Bam, bam, bam, bam.* They sounded like thunderclaps. Until, near the close of the workout, Gretzky slipped into a corner and disappeared. Concentrating on Jari Kurri, Whitney half-stepped out of the mouth of the goal to minimise Kurri's angle. An instant later, the puck plunked off the goalie's back into the net.

'If you take your eye off Gretzky,' Whitney told me, 'he'll bank it off your skate, your back, your helmet, your wife.'

I congratulated Floyd, all the same, on the many wonderful

saves he had made. 'I didn't even see some of them,' Whitney said. 'Gretz was aiming for my glove.'

CHECKMATE

When Bobby Fischer suddenly returned from Howard Hughes land, it was a chess story to most of you. It was a journalism story to some of us. Maybe Bill Nack would find his ending.

Nack was the graceful voice of horse racing for *Sports Illustrated*, a chess degenerate on the side. Some years ago, he got to wondering, 'What really happened to Fischer?' And a quest began.

Off and on for years, Nack picked through broken bottles and desperate hotels for signs of history's youngest grand master, who overwhelmed Soviet champion Boris Spassky and disappeared.

The ending in chess is often weird. More than a hundred years ago, Paul Morphy, the only other American world champion, roamed the streets of New Orleans, muttering to himself in French, 'He will plant the banner of Castille upon the walls of Madrid, amidst the cries of the conquered city, and the little king will go away looking very sheepish.'

Morphy died of apoplexy in his 40s, surrounded by his collection of women's shoes.

All the same, Nack was unprepared for how odd the Fischer trail would be. Along the way, he learned that Bobby, a Brooklyn Jew, was a spiteful anti-Semite. Another thing: suspicious of government technology, Fischer reportedly had all of the metal fillings removed from his teeth, lest they be employed as transmitters.

Chess's object is to kill the king. The dominant piece is the queen. Fischer never knew his father. His mother, heartbreakingly enough, was named Regina. As Nack closed in, he felt increasingly depressed.

★ DANCIN' WITH SONNY LISTON

Because nothing makes a man look over his shoulder more than looking for a man looking over his shoulder, Nack sprayed his hair grey and donned old clothes (even older than sportswriters' clothes) to stake out the Los Angeles Public Library, where Fischer sightings had been reported.

Finally, just before closing time, there he stood, more tattered than Nack, bearded, balding and heavier than his photographs. But Bill didn't confront him, or so much as speak to him. At the end of the day, he hadn't the heart. For several blocks, Nack followed the strange, shambling, rolling figure, then let him go.

Racing to the typewriter, Bill wrote everything he knew, starting with the fact that, contrary to the most persistent rumour of all, Fischer was alive. For years, those of us with bloodier teeth ridiculed Nack for not going for the jugular and making sure.

We succeeded in planting just the germ of a doubt. When the senior tours came to chess, and Fischer–Spassky II was announced for Montenegro, Bill carried that doubt with him on the *Orient Express*, from Vienna to Belgrade by way of Budapest.

From Belgrade, he flew over the mountains to Tivat on the Adriatic and strolled across a footbridge to Sveti Stefan and the truth. Nack and the world waited for Bobby to enter the hall of mirrors.

With a shambling, rolling walk, Fischer came into the room, bearded, balding and heavier than his photographs. Nack smiled. In a news conference, Fischer unleashed a diatribe against 'world Jewry' and the conspiratorial government of the United States.

At dinner later, reporters queued up in the vain hope of a question-and-answer session. Fischer looked past them at Nack and mouthed the words *Sports Illustrated*. Bill made a little bow, and that was that.

9

Use Your Own Trick Plays First

The first pro football locker room I ever stepped into was the Colts' locker room in Baltimore's Memorial Stadium after a game with the Chicago Bears. I was taking a long look around when I felt a tap on my shoulder. It was the legendary receiver Raymond Berry.

'You look a little lost,' he said in his Texas drawl, and I introduced myself. 'Who d'you want to talk to?' he asked.

'Unitas.'

Wading into the crowd of reporters clogging Unitas's locker, Berry dragged out the quarterback and introduced us, saying, 'John, this is a friend of mine, Tom Callahan. He wants to ask you a few questions.'

'Hey, Tommy,' Unitas said, pulling out a small milkman's stool and sitting down in the middle of the room. Berry kicked me a stool, and we started in. Nobody else came near.

Some years later, in Winter Haven, Florida, I was trying to interview Ted Williams. Of course, you couldn't interview Williams. He interviewed you.

'So you were in Baltimore for a while then?' Williams asked, continuing his interrogation. 'Do you know Unitas?'

'A little bit.'

'Let me ask you something,' he said. 'If Unitas is standing at the line of scrimmage, and there's an explosion in the stadium, and half of the grandstands burst into flame, what does he do?'

'He runs the play,' I said.

'That's God-given!' Williams shouted. 'That's Johnny U., all right! You do know him! What was it you wanted to ask me, Tommy?'

With one foot balanced on the running board of a Hupmobile in Canton, Ohio, a former Rose Bowl MVP and New York Yankees right-fielder named George Halas began to invent the National Football League in 1920. Red Grange would carry the mail. Cash & Carry Pyle would deliver it. But essentially it was a coach's game. It belonged to them.

After Halas, the next proprietor was an Ohio schoolmaster, Paul Brown, who paced the sidelines in a wide-brimmed hat and a long overcoat, looking like the homicide inspector viewing the body. Among other things, he put the classroom in pro football.

A cold little man with a pointy nose, Brown thought of almost everything first. To mollify mothers, wives and dentists, he hit on the idea of face masks across the beams of the helmets and, through Jerry Riddell of the Riddell Sporting Goods Company, filed a patent. 'There were years,' Brown purred late in a long career, 'when I did about as well from that as from anything else.' His Cleveland Browns, partly named for him, were the leading survivors of the All-America Football Conference, a failed rival to the NFL. In the NFL opener of 1950, much laughter accompanied Brown's motley crew (fullback Marion Motley, that is, not to mention quarterback Otto Graham) to Philadelphia, where the world champion Eagles and star runner Steve Van Buren waited in bemused ambush.

Brown's pre-game speech was terse and typical: 'Just think,' he said dryly, 'in a minute you'll get to *touch* Steve Van Buren.'

As the Browns stampeded out of the locker room, Lou 'The Toe' Groza nearly kicked the door off its hinges. As a matter of fact, Van Buren was injured, although not as badly as the Eagles (and the rest of the NFL) were insulted, 35–10. 'The Browns are an aerial circus,' grumped Philadelphia coach Greasy Neale, who had never seen such passing. 'That ain't football. That's basketball.'

For the rematch near the close of the season, Van Buren was back but nothing else was different. Well, one thing was. 'Do you know how many passes we threw?' Brown asked me years later with the sigh of a nostalgic executioner. He held up his hand in the OK sign. 'Zero,' he said. 'The field was muddy. We elected to run over them this time.'

So settled were the champion Browns in 1951 that only two rookies made the club. Don Shula made the travelling team and Carl Taseff the 'taxi' squad. They were defensive backs of similar bearing and build, both from Cleveland's John Carroll University, and Brown had a hard time telling them apart. 'Nice tackle, Taseff,' the coach barked one day at practice after Motley was upended.

'The name's "Shula"!' Shula bounced up to shout. 'S-h-u-l-a!'

A dreadful silence fell like Motley on the field. The temperature dropped, too, about 25 degrees. The veterans were shivering. They expected the ground to breach and swallow the rookie.

But Brown smiled like a razor blade and the sun reappeared. 'I'll try to remember,' he said tartly.

Shula would be the best of a legion of coaches Brown passed down and around. The impression was that Brown's assistants proliferated as head coaches throughout football. But, in truth, it was his players, such as Lou Saban in Buffalo, Bud Grant in Minnesota and Chuck Noll in Pittsburgh. Any assistant coaches who walked away from Brown, starting as far back as the Colts' (and Jets') Weeb Ewbank, were forever encased in icicles.

I knew Brown in his second coming, with the Cincinnati Bengals, when I was the sports columnist for the morning *Enquirer*. Sort of knew him. 'Do you know me so well?' he asked after a pointed column. 'Does anyone?' I replied. He liked words and he had a kind of stony charm. 'I used to teach English,' he would say. 'I can define a gerund. Can you?'

But he could be frigid to the point of frostbite.

One day, during a thaw, we were chatting beside the practice field. On the opposite sideline, his son Mike, the Bengals' bald, bookish-looking legal counsel, was playing catch with one of the receivers, Chip Myers, throwing surprisingly tight spirals. I got along with Mike. He was about the only one in the front office who understood that the relationship between the writers and the team was necessarily adversarial.

'Mike can throw a little,' I said to Paul.

'Oh, he was a pretty good college quarterback,' Brown said, 'at Dartmouth. Probably as good as what we [the Cleveland Browns] had at the time, Milt Plum' – on Brown's lips, 'Milt Plum' sounded like 'bubonic plague' – 'and I never knew a kid who wanted to play pro football more than Mike. But that wasn't in my plans. He was going to be the lawyer.'

Continuing, Brown said, 'A report came to me that some team or other was thinking of taking a late-round flyer on Mike. I put the word out: "If you don't, we won't. Pass it on."'

'Let me get this straight,' I said, closing my notebook, making sure he knew this wasn't for the paper. 'You never saw a kid who wanted to play pro football more than your own son, so you made sure he didn't?' Brown didn't talk to me again that season.

One of Brown's assistants, quietly his most indispensable aide, was an offensive theorist from California, Bill Walsh, whose football traced from Al Davis in Oakland, meaning from Sid Gillman in San Diego. Again, it's a coach's game. Anyway, Walsh knew how to complete a pass.

Several communication levels above the average football coach, he could talk about other things besides the game. He could even express misgivings about football and about some of the people who played it.

Early in their 1970s expansion days, the Bengals employed a line coach named Tom Bass, a hulking, fearsome figure who could have portrayed Taras Bulba with very little make-up. He was the one who recommended Walsh. Contrary to appearances, Bass was a sensitive man, a poet. His post on the sideline was too near to the violence and, in time, Bass literally turned his back on the field. Walsh was a little like that but insulated up in the booth, whispering logarithms into a headset. By then, Brown couldn't sketch a whole play. (Oh, maybe a 'draw' play.) The game had become increasingly, incredibly, complicated. Sometimes Paul would posture at the blackboard with a stick of chalk. The players' eyes would roll merrily.

But that didn't mean Brown wasn't in total charge of his team. He had axioms and the team lived by them, such as, 'Use your own trick plays first.' For many years, Brown's favourite trick play was something called 'the triple pass'. Brown's pronouncements were absolute. 'Greg Cook will be going in on the next series,' he'd call up top to tell Walsh.

'What?'

'Greg Cook is our quarterback.'

Painstakingly, Walsh had just finished lifting limited Sam Wyche up to a tolerable level of inefficiency. Walsh enjoyed mining and maximising the simple skills of a Wyche, Virgil Carter or Guy Benjamin as much as releasing the compound-complex talents of a Ken Anderson, Dan Fouts or Joe Montana. But Greg Cook was their quarterback. On the cusp of Brown's second merger (this time, the NFL and AFL), really in the only season he ever played, Cook was both the Rookie of the Year and the Most Valuable Player of the American Football League. During a late-season victory against Kansas City, Walsh called a roll-out pass requiring the halfback to cut across the formation and handle outside linebacker Bobby Bell. Bell blitzed off the corner, flattened the blocker and flipped Cook on his shoulder. That was the end of Cook's rotator cuff. For all practical purposes, that was the end of Cook. Walsh still broods about the call.

Weary of waiting for Brown to retire (deluding himself, with Brown's sly encouragement, that he was the coach on-deck), by the end of the '70s Walsh was tossing his hat into almost every open ring. But all of them were intercepted by Paul. It was Davis of the Raiders who whispered to Walsh that lukewarm recommendations flowing from Brown were scotching his applications. Like Mr Roberts on the bridge (Cagney could have played Brown one-handed), Walsh was afraid that the war was passing him by. Most of Bill's contemporaries, it seemed, were head coaches in colleges. Few of them made more money than he; none had more responsibility or a greater outlet for creativity. But at least they were their own men.

Youthful, although older than he seemed, Walsh had taken quite a while just getting his hands on the ball. He grew up in the south central section of Los Angeles, close enough to the University of Southern California to ball-boy for the Trojans. The first football game he ever saw, the one that enchanted him permanently, was a 13–0 USC loss to the University of Notre Dame, quarterbacked by Heisman Trophy winner Angelo Bertelli ('The Springfield Rifle'). Walsh dreamed of being the quarterback.

His father, an auto-plant labourer who wound up with his own body-and-fender shop, moved around enough during Bill's teenage years to land him at three different high schools and pretty much kill his chances of ever being the signal caller. He was always catching up to a new system. This would work for him later on.

Ultimately, Walsh was permitted to take a few snaps for San Mateo Community College, but he was moved back to end by San Jose State. After college, a series of fellowships and apprenticeships and internships around the California capitals of the Pac-8 and the NFL supplied him a postgraduate football education. For a few years, he coached a high school team. One Continental League season in San Jose, he tutored a developmental squad that was co-financed by the Raiders and 49ers.

Short of glamorous credentials but wormy with ideas, Walsh moved up to the expansion Bengals. 'Nobody gave me the quarterbacks,' he said. 'I just took them.'

It was tremendous pressure and tremendous fun. He built Ken Anderson of Augustana (Illinois) College completely from scratch. But near the end in Cincinnati, Bill was given to soft laments, uttered late at night, usually on the road. One of these almost drew him into a fistfight with a Brown loyalist who'd had a few drinks and was weary of Walsh's Hamlet. 'I'm not going through with this,' Walsh said in an alley outside the hotel bar. He went to bed. (At Fort Ord in the Army, besides playing on the post football team, Walsh had also been a boxer.)

That night, he had trouble sleeping. But it wasn't the next day's game that was keeping him awake. He had invented (in the Midwest, incidentally) something that would come to be known as the 'West Coast Offence'. But at that moment he didn't know whether it would come to be known at all. Walsh had been changing his sport and no one knew it.

Brown's final game as coach – though only he knew that at the time – was a 31–28 play-off loss against the Raiders in Oakland. I was there, but I missed the sign. Meeting the press afterwards, Brown didn't seem all that disappointed to me. I couldn't put my finger on what was different, but I knew something was. On the following New Year's Day (I was typing away in the press box at the Rose Bowl), Paul issued a curt statement that he had retired from coaching to concentrate on general managing, and that his longest-standing assistant, 'Tiger' Bill Johnson, was the new head coach. Neither Brown nor Johnson was available that day for comment. Cruelly, it fell to Walsh to service the local media, to provide cheerful soundbites to all of the television people who came in waves to his home. He lied politely and never showed his despair. Shortly after that, I received a telephone call from Walsh. 'I'd like to take you into my confidence,' he said.

Tommy Prothro of the Chargers had offered him the job of offensive coordinator in San Diego and, lateral move or not, Walsh was inclined to take it. But he still imagined he had an outside shot at the vacant head coaching job with the New York Jets. Al Davis was campaigning for him. But time was short. Lou Holtz was secretly in New York City that afternoon being interviewed by Jet executive Jim Kensil.

'I just have a feeling,' Walsh said, 'that, in New York, dealing with the media is a major concern. Would you call Kensil and vouch for me?' I was stunned. At first, all I could think to say was, 'What makes you want the Jets?'

'I'd like a shot at Joe Namath at the end of his career,' he said softly. I couldn't believe that this man who knew so much about the game knew so little about the game. 'Bill,' I said, 'if Kensil somehow found out we hated each other, that might help you. If he knew you told me about Holtz, it'd kill you. Now it's going to take all of my restraint not to call Dave Anderson [the *New York Times*] and tell him about Holtz and not to call Jerry Magee [the *San Diego Union*] and tell him about you.'

He got it; we tried to laugh. He knew everything I was

saying better than I did, but he was that desperate. Holtz got the job and, I don't think it's unfair to say, botched it spectacularly.

When Walsh told Paul and Mike he was going to San Diego, they double-teamed him, alternately tossing money and threats. Walsh's Bengals contract was up the following week, but Paul said that didn't matter. This was tampering. Get it straight, they told him. You're not going anywhere.

Walsh broke down into tears. They mistakenly thought he was crying in disappointment at being passed over. But his emotions were far more complicated than that, like his offence. He gathered himself, smiled at Paul and said goodbye. Some days later, Walsh happened to be with Prothro when Brown telephoned the Chargers' head coach. Tommy motioned for Walsh to get on the extension, and, unknown to Brown, Walsh silently listened to what a backstabber he was and what a mistake it would be ever to trust him with the offence or anything else. Walsh and Prothro looked at each other with the sad eyes of the industry.

After dressing Dan Fouts for the Hall of Fame, Walsh moved to the head coaching job at Stanford, where at last he was running his own show at the age of 47. Before Walsh turned 50, 49ers owner Eddie DeBartolo called. San Francisco wasn't just a depressed team; it was the French Foreign Legion. A big chunk of the future had just been bartered by imperial general manager Joe Thomas for the celebrated remains of O.J. Simpson.

Walsh's first condition to the 49ers was that Thomas had to go. Making a list of all of the young comers ready to be GMs, Walsh couldn't persuade George Young, Ernie Accorsi or any of the others to risk their careers and accompany him. So, Walsh took on the entire task. 'I was confident about the on-the-field part,' he told me much later. 'The other stuff scared the hell out of me.' His last duty for Stanford was the

Bluebonnet Bowl against the University of Georgia. 'We were supposed to have this high-powered, NFL-style offence,' Walsh recalled, 'but we were down, 16–0, at half. As the score increased, the Georgia players began making effeminate gestures at us from the sideline.' Walsh adjusted the meter of his offence, shortening the pass patterns and turning away from the ends in favour of backfield receivers. The Bulldogs did not adjust their heavy-blitzing defence. Stanford gutted and cleaned them, 25–22. That same day, only sometimes-starter Joe Montana came off the Notre Dame bench during a frigid Cotton Bowl to retrieve a similar situation against the University of Houston. Walsh read the accounts with interest.

A week before his inaugural pro draft, Bill personally auditioned Montana and a UCLA high-hurdler named James Owens in Los Angeles. Montana was rather slight and his arm was not extraordinary. But his feet were nimble; he could dance. And he seemed to be able to think.

The 49ers selected Owens in the first round. They had no second-round pick. In the third, knowing all along that Montana would still be there, Walsh finally called his name. Three years later, they were in the Super Bowl – against the Bengals.

To get to that game, the 49ers beat the New York Giants and the Dallas Cowboys in the play-offs. By then, I was at *Time* magazine. Guessing, *Time* decided to put Montana on the cover Super Bowl week, provided, of course, the 49ers were involved. I went out to San Francisco for the Giants game and stayed for the Cowboys.

Because of the weather in the Bay Area, the 49ers moved to a hotel in Anaheim for the week. At Walsh's request, Montana came to my room at night to talk. He seemed like a nice kid but especially he seemed like a kid. 'I'm just doing all those things I dreamed of as a kid,' he said. 'That's what you do. Before it ever happens on the field, it's played in your mind.'

This was Montana's first year as the starter. The previous season, Steve DeBerg had set an NFL record for completions. But, the instant Montana was ready, DeBerg was transferred out of town. Walsh truly was a pup out of Brown. Funnily enough, Montana missed DeBerg. He missed the competition, not on the field as much as in the bathroom. Roommates, they played checkers on the black-and-white tiles of the lavatory floor. They played video games, they played cards, they pitched nickels. They never stopped competing. That was Montana. The thing he missed most about Notre Dame was the intramural basketball league. He did not put me in mind of Johnny Unitas. One of San Francisco's offensive linemen insisted to me that, despite the new game's kaleidoscopic formations and whirlwind substitutions that complicate and limit the modern quarterback's options, Montana had an old quarterback's presence and command. 'Only on the field,' he said. 'It's hard to explain. I wish I could think of an example. Off the field, he's a dormitory rat, a teenybopper. But he turns into Bobby Layne, I promise you. Before Joe's done, he's going to have six Super Bowls and five wives.'

The Cowboy game, the last step to the 49ers' first Super Bowl, came down to that renowned 'catch' by Dwight Clark in the back of the end zone. Paul Brown told people it was a haphazard fling; in fact, it was a practised last option. As few recall, the Cowboys still had a drive left in them. By that time, as usual, the writers had milled down from the press box to the field. Waiting on the sideline in a blazer was the retired Dallas quarterback Roger Staubach, whom I knew a little. As both teams lined up for the final push, he said, 'You're the tensest-looking one out here.'

'Roger,' I said. 'This is the first football game I've cared who wins since Gino Marchetti retired.'

I'd written a rather long story that could be rather useless. But the Cowboys' drive ended on a fumble.

When the locker room doors opened afterward, the offensive lineman I had been talking to was motioning wildly. He had thought of an illustration. It wouldn't fit in *Time* magazine, but it helped me see Montana as Unitas, Layne or Staubach.

All week, Dallas defensive skyscraper Ed 'Too Tall' Jones had been asserting, 'We don't have to worry about the deep pass. This guy can't throw deep.' (Essentially, he was right.)

But, early on, when Montana threw a 60-yard pass to Freddie Solomon, Joe turned to Too Tall and asked, 'Deep enough for you, motherfucker?' 'My heart dropped,' said the 49er lineman. 'We had to block Jones the rest of the game. Joe is always ridiculing the pass rushers this way. "Nice to see you, boys," he'll say after a sack. "I been wondering where the fuck you've been." But, I'll tell you something: this time, Too Tall quit. He flat quit.' In the Super Bowl two weeks later, against the Bengals, Montana handed off to Ricky Patton running right, who handed off to Solomon reversing left, who flipped the ball back to Montana, who passed it to Charlie Young for a first down. From the sideline, Walsh allowed himself just a quick glance at the reflective glass atop the Pontiac Silverdome, behind which Brown sat, looking more like the body than the homicide inspector.

Walsh had used his own trick play first, and it was the old 'triple pass'. The 49ers won and kept winning. Walsh won three Super Bowls in San Francisco and then handed the system off to others to win more. As the latest custodian of the game, he was cast in bronze alongside Halas, Brown and all of the other fabled pro football coaches in Canton, Ohio.

Epilogues are untidy, but Walsh couldn't help himself. After a victory lap at Stanford and a short pass at TV commentating (encountered with the NBC Olympic party on a boat in the Barcelona harbour, he told me, 'I know what you're doing here. What am I doing here?'), Walsh reclaimed the GM chair in San Francisco as the century ran out.

Salary-cap mortgages and a 38-year-old well-concussed quarterback (Steve Young) assured the 49ers their most difficult patch since the dawn of the Bill Walsh era. Walsh didn't pretend otherwise.

Sitting in his office in the 2000 pre-season, he was the only one excited about a kid quarterback, Jeff Garcia of San Jose State, just back from exile in Canada. Bill said, 'When I was out of the league, before Garcia went north, I tried to sell him to one NFL team after another. Most didn't even answer my letter.' But, furtively looking around, the way Al Davis used to canvass the area for spies, Walsh whispered, 'He's got instincts. Take a look at him at practice today.'

'All I ever learn at practice,' I said, 'is not to go to practice.' He laughed. 'I remember,' he said. 'P.B. used to call you "The Phantom". He'd say, "That guy never comes to practice."'

But this wasn't entirely true.

Years before, during lunch at a Bengals pre-season camp, I asked Brown if he had any bright ideas for a column. He cracked a joke in reply. But later, when the players were back on the field for the second session, and I was typing in a dormitory room, there was a barely discernible scratch at the door. The second time I heard it, I turned the knob; there stood Paul.

'I didn't mean to be impertinent earlier,' he said in his arch way. 'I've been thinking about what you asked me, and I guess if I were a columnist today, I wouldn't be writing about all of the great things Virgil Carter did for us in the past. I'd be taking a good, hard look at this young fellow, Ken Anderson. I'd be especially interested in how tall he stands in the pocket and I'd take particular notice of how the other players on the offence respond to him.'

'So what you're telling me,' I said to Walsh, 'is that, despite what I've been reading in the *Chronicle*, Garcia is the 49ers' quarterback.'

'He may not be the quarterback of the future,' Bill said, 'but, if he can handle following a Hall of Famer [Young] and the best ever [Montana], he's got a real shot. He can do a lot of the same things Montana and Young could, just not as fast.'

'"Not as fast" doesn't sound so good,' I said.

'That's where we are now.'

Walsh was also honest about the camp's celebrated reclamation project, runner Lawrence Phillips, late of Nebraska, St Louis, and assorted police blotters, finally down to his last chance.

'A lot of people here are mad at me for bringing him in, but maybe he can help us a little.' As it turned out, he either couldn't or wouldn't. 'Forgetting the sociology,' Walsh said, 'I'm not sure he's good enough.' The sociology has always been there. 'There's a dark side to the sport, there really is,' Walsh said. 'Even more than there is in society, I think.'

In Cleveland, Coach Brown tolerated a superstar who liked to put cigarettes out on women. He was a hell of a player. 'Some play football well,' Walsh said, 'because they are incredibly cruel people. Part of it may be steroids and their insidious side effects. I've had wives complain to me that they no longer know the husbands they're living with. But a lot of it is just simple brutishness that starts on the field and drips over into life.' How dark has it gotten? 'Well, I went to a hotel parking lot once where one of our players was under a car being beaten up by two drug dealers. One of our leaders. He was trying to buy cocaine for a team party.'

Cocaine is an element that has to be broken down by today's coaches, like game films.

Walsh said, 'I don't know whether the sensitive coach is any improvement over the old hard-rock guy who would line up all of the cocaine users and shoot them [read: Vince Lombardi]. Neither one seems to do much good.' Coaches know the drug's effect on sleep and nutrition, and at practice they can guess which players have been up all night. 'I can pick them out,' Walsh said. 'One, two, three, four. It's not the biggest part of football's story, but it's the saddest part.'

He couldn't always pick them out.

'Remember Hollywood Henderson?'

Sure. Thomas 'Hollywood' Henderson. Linebacker. Brilliant athlete. Talker. He was the one who, before a Cowboys–Steelers Super Bowl, said Terry Bradshaw 'couldn't spell cat if you spotted him the c and the a'. 'Thomas had a gorgeous wife, Wyetta,' Walsh said, 'a concert pianist. They came to our house for dinner. His wife gave my daughter, Elizabeth, a piano lesson. All through dinner, Thomas kept excusing himself to go to the bathroom. I was so stupid. He was snorting cocaine in my home. We took a walk afterward. He was totally incoherent. He wanted more money.'

Eventually, Henderson took Walsh to places he never thought a coach had to go. 'Two secretaries here had a fistfight over him, if you can believe it. They tore each other's dresses off. Before we waived him, I had to dress him – he was zonked out on the floor of the locker room – so we could film him practising in case he later tried to claim injury and sue us. We held a completely phony workout just long enough for three cameras to film Hollywood Henderson.' The Hollywood Henderson Follies. 'He plagued Houston and Miami after us. He has come through it, though. He's OK now. Thomas gives anti-drug talks to kids today, calls me now and again. It sounds funny, but I like him.' In a twenty-first-century denouement either too good to be true or too scary to be believed, Hollywood Henderson, reformed addict, won the Texas lottery and $28 million.

Walsh stepped down as the 49ers GM in 2001, at 69. Stepped aside may be more accurate. Two years later, as a vice-president, he was still dipping his fingers into the 49er game plans. He also stayed involved in the comings and goings of coaches. He continued to be embedded in football.

How would Walsh describe a life of football now?

'There's the cruelty, the meanness, the brutality, the volatility, the insensitivity,' he began briskly. But then, slowing down, he said, 'There's the beauty and the glory, the sense of artistic accomplishment, the incredible fellowship.'

What was the low point?

'Low points, you mean. After the big loss, when you're drained physically, mentally and emotionally, and there's nothing left of you, and you kneel down for the prayer and you can't get up, and somehow you make it back to the coaches' room and just break down, sobbing.'

Over a game.

And the high point?

'Oh, personal satisfactions.'

His most personal ones are the coaches he has passed down and around, assistants more than players, like Mike Holmgren and Brian Billick, and particularly the black coaches, like Dennis Green and Ray Rhodes. 'Years ago, when I was pondering how we could pay for a minority intern system,' Walsh said, 'it hit me. Put Eddie DeBartolo's name on it. Put his name on it and Eddie will pay for anything.'

By 2003, the Walsh coaching tree had branched out to embrace Herman Edwards, Marvin Lewis, Tony Dungy and Tyrone Willingham, and the fruit of it included ten of the past twenty-two Super Bowl championships.

In his 70s, Walsh smiled as easily as ever, at himself especially. 'A few days ago,' he told me, 'I was at the blackboard, lecturing on "prevent" defence for twenty minutes before I realised I only had ten men on my defence.' When he did realise it, he spun around and looked at the players, whose eyes were rolling merrily. Of course he thought of Paul. 'Just think, in a minute you'll get to *touch* Steve Van Buren.' . . .

'S-h-u-l-a.' . . . 'Greg Cook is our quarterback.' . . . 'Use your own trick plays first.'

The 49ers who joined him in laughter could not have begun to understand.

It was Sunday afternoon, but the Buffalo Bills weren't playing until the following evening, and O.J. Simpson was lounging in the hotel room of the Bills' public relations man, Bud Thalman. That Monday night in the rain, Simpson would play one of the most memorable games of his spectacular career.

The topic being kicked around the room that day, and the league that year, was: who was better? The retired Jim Brown or the rampaging O.J. Simpson? Turning to me, Simpson asked, 'Who do you think was better? Me or Brown?' 'Gale Sayers,' I said. He laughed. (I promise you, Jim Brown wouldn't have laughed.) 'You know, you're probably right,' he said. Maybe that's why we liked him.

10

Setting Trees and Striking Lampposts

At the age of 16, when I was 6 ft 2 in. tall and could pass for 17, I spent a summer in summer stock carrying spears, rounding out crowd scenes, and playing a few bit parts. But my real function was setting trees and striking lampposts, or doing anything else the director directed, which is how I came to make love to Marilyn Maxwell.

She was attempting Judy Holliday's role in *Bells Are Ringing* opposite Hal Linden, Sydney Chaplin's Broadway understudy, who would grow up to be TV's Barney Miller. At the overture each night, at least to a 16-year-old boy, Marilyn looked stunningly beautiful. But this was summertime in Baltimore, in a tent, in the round, and by intermission her honey-blonde hair was a mop. She declined to wear her eyeglasses anywhere near the stage, although without them during the changes she was as blind as Mrs Magoo. By the end of the first week, her injuries from bumping into the scenery had reached a point where I was directed to set the lamppost and strike Marilyn Maxwell. She was a mess and I loved her.

I was appointed to drive Marilyn home each night to her hotel. Literally I carried her in my arms to bed and, until the final night of the run, chastely sat and listened to her dissertations on middle age. After playing the 'other woman' in a lot of B movies and touring a few war fronts with Bob Hope, she had landed what she imagined to be the lead role in the television series *Bus Stop*. But all the writers seemed to want her to do was pour coffee. To the boy sitting on the edge of her bed, she advised savouring the romantic processes of beginning and building because the phase that follows, the maintaining and upkeeping, can be a bitter time for desperate thoughts of lives squandered and dreams betrayed. We made love.

Luckily, she knew how. This time, I was the one bumping into the scenery. More than a few years later, colleague Dave Kindred asked me to sub for him in a Super Bowl golf tournament and I arrived at the first tee to find one of my partners extending his hand: Hal Linden.

'Mr Kindred, I presume,' he said.

'I'm Callahan, his understudy.'

He laughed.

'Dave's sort of my Sydney Chaplin,' I went on, and he stopped laughing.

'How do you know that?'

'Oh, I'm an old actor myself,' I said, propping a ball up on a tee and staring into the clouds. 'I delivered the flowers to Marilyn Maxwell in the second act.'

WILT

Two waves of guests were invited to Wilt Chamberlain's new home, Ursa Major (The Big Dipper), and Wilt was hurrying the first section along like a White House tour guide. 'One of my closest friends is Bill Shoemaker, the jockey,' he said. 'I told the architects I didn't want Shoe to feel like he was Jack at the Beanstalk. I think they pulled it off quite well.' Trooping through stately door frames, passing by oversized furniture, peeking into gargantuan showers, I felt like Stuart Little.

Wilt was wearing a yellow jumpsuit that, he couldn't have realised, made him appear 12 feet tall. He never wanted to be that tall. He hated the inevitable sobriquet 'Wilt the Stilt', but 'Dipper' was embroidered on his shirt cuffs. Neither of Chamberlain's parents and none of his siblings were unusually tall. In West Philadelphia, Wilton Norman grew up, and up, always taking tender care not to damage his more fragile playmates. Wilt's entire life, he was the antithesis of a bully.

For a time in the National Basketball Association, Chamberlain listed himself at 7 ft $1^1/_{16}$, obviously to imply that, at least at some point, he had been precisely measured, although I doubt he ever was. Even during lay-up drills, Wilt eschewed dunks in favour of slouching 'finger rolls' that were calculated to keep him as close as possible to the floor.

One sleepy morning in Inglewood's 'Fabulous Forum', he stood absolutely flat-footed underneath the basket, reached up, grabbed the rim and shook it, yawning and stretching like a bear coming out of hibernation. 'Ahhhhhhhhhhhhhh!' he said. Suddenly remembering himself, Wilt let the hoop go with a reverberating 'boing-de-ridium' and glanced around in horror to see if he had been observed. Bill Sharman, the Laker coach, one of the best free-throw shooters in basketball history, had instituted mandatory foul-shooting sessions on game days. Of course, Chamberlain was notoriously wretched from the line, whether he scooped the ball two-handed from between his long legs or shot-putted it from the far left of the stripe or the far right or, illogically enough, from a couple of feet behind it.

All the same, there isn't a historic missed free throw for which Chamberlain is remembered. He made quite a few of them that mattered. The season he averaged 50 points a game, many people predicted: 'One of these nights, if Wilt hits his foul shots, he'll score a hundred points.' And that's just what happened. Twenty-eight for thirty-two from the line, he had one hundred exactly. Shaquille O'Neal could stand there forever trying to make twenty-eight of thirty-two.

Tired of being called a 'gunner', Chamberlain set out to

establish a record for assists, and did. He could be remarkably single-minded. But basketball as a whole eluded him.

His most telling record wasn't the 100-point game or the 4,000-point season or the 35 straight shots he made or the 33 straight games he won or the 55 rebounds (55 rebounds!) he gathered on a single night against Bill Russell. The key record, the one that opens the lock, is that, in 14 pro seasons, Chamberlain never fouled out of a game.

'That's what may stop you, Willie,' Sharman's old Celtic backcourt mate Bob Cousy whispered as the Lakers were pursuing a second straight title. Six fouls disqualified a player. After four, Wilt essentially ceased playing. It was more important to him not to be an ogre even than it was to be a winner.

If he had been a different sort of guy, guards wouldn't have dared jump up and toss an arm around his neck when they were 'giving' a foul. Walt Bellamy, Zelmo Beatty, Willis Reed, Wes Unseld, Nate Thurmond, Kareem Abdul-Jabbar, Russell – certainly Russell – would have punched their hearts out. Standing 6 ft 9 in. or so, Russell was just that much smaller and therefore just that much more agile than Chamberlain. Still, were Wilt a different sort of guy, he'd have killed Russell.

Chamberlain had his flashes of anger. He stuck Gus 'Honeycomb' Johnson in the basket once. How strong was Gus? No one who ever shook his hand has yet completely let go of the sensation. In a media game once, Johnson wrapped one finger in the leg of my shorts and I couldn't move either foot. Wilt scared Sam Jones so badly that Sam ran to the bench and picked up a chair. Bob Ferry fled all of the way into the mezzanine. Unseld has a film clip of this that he pulls out for guests as eagerly as a new father displaying baby pictures. The legend is that Alex Hannum, the tough-guy coach of Wilt's championship team in Philadelphia, once shoved Chamberlain into a men's room, saying, 'If you aren't going to respect me as a coach, at least you're going to respect me as a man.' As the story goes, Wilt knocked him out.

Delicately, I put this to Hannum once. He didn't deny it. But Alex loved Wilt and Wilt loved him. 'Alex is a loquacious man,' was all Chamberlain would say when I brought it up.

Wilt devoured sports, all sports, and he knew all of the names and numbers. At the Montreal Olympics, Red Smith, Jack Murphy and I bumped into him in a restaurant. 'Have you been watching the basketball?' Smith asked. 'Not just the basketball, Red,' Chamberlain said, a bit annoyed. The city was vibrating with the perfect performance of Romanian gymnast Nadia Comaneci, and Wilt was a little steamed about it.

'It's the same old thing,' he said. 'You guys always go for the tiniest and the cutest. Last time it was Olga Korbut, even though Lyudmila Tourischeva was better.'

Who else in the NBA remembered Lyudmila Tourischeva's name?

Not just track, basketball and volleyball, all games came naturally to Chamberlain, whose pass-catching ability excited football coach Hank Stram until, typically, Wilt said he wanted to play quarterback.

Wilt also wanted to fight Muhammad Ali, and when the talks grew semi-serious, Ali was the one who demurred. Angelo Dundee climbed up on a chair and said, 'Hit me in the head, Champ.'

Muhammad thought it over and replied, 'Let's see him fight Doug Jones first.' Wilt just laughed.

On the morning of a sixth game of a championship series with the Knicks that the Lakers had to win merely to force a seventh game back in New York, Chamberlain showed up sleepily for Sharman's shoot-around. Sticking his head through a swinging door into a Forum lounge, where several writers were having coffee, Wilt said pointedly, to no one in particular: 'Any-body-who-owes-me-money, have-it-here-to-night.'

The series was over.

'Here,' he said, handing me a pen and paper, not five minutes after the long season ended. 'Write down your number. My volleyball team is touring this summer.'

The tour of Ursa Major ended in the bedroom, where a bed the size of a small polo field was covered with a mammoth spread made entirely of the soft noses of wolves. This was the part of the housewarming that moved the story to the front page and cost Chamberlain the wolf vote.

But, in the upset of the waning century, when Wilt's heart gave out suddenly at 63, not even the Sierra Club had a bad word to say about him. Teammates and opponents alike cried and laughed with sadness and affection. Russell, of all people, praised him to the rafters. Everybody, it turned out, had loved Goliath.

He would have been so thrilled to hear it.

Very little time was spent totalling up either the championships (two) or the little blonde Kim Novaks in pigtails (thousands, including Kim Novak). He was just the strongest and most amazing athlete and man anyone had ever seen. And he was a good guy.

Chamberlain drove a pink Bentley. One time, he was leading Hannum and a few of us to a San Francisco restaurant, but even with the rental car floored, the Bentley was flying farther and farther ahead, until inevitably Alex was pulled over by a trooper.

Copping a basketball plea, Hannum showed the officer his licence while rattling off his Bay Area credits. Meanwhile, Wilt doubled back not once, but twice, whooshing by like a pink rocket. The second time, the trooper almost – just almost – threw his flashlight at the car.

'Who the hell is that?' he said.

'Superman,' somebody whispered.

SO LONG, TOBY

'I never talked to Callahan,' Elvin Hayes swore to owner Bob Breitbard, general manager Pete Newell, coach Alex Hannum and all of his fellow Rockets players, summoned to an emergency session at the San Diego Sports Arena. 'I didn't even know he was on the trip.'

'Then we're going to have a press conference,' Breitbard said angrily, 'and you're going to call him a liar.'

'Good,' Elvin said.

Public relations man Bob King was dispatched to summon all of the local media to George Pernicano's restaurant at noon.

The day before, in the middle of a bus ride from San Diego to Los Angeles for a Laker game, Hayes left his seat in the back to fill the one beside me.

'I'm tired of playing with these losers,' he said after a minute or so, and I glanced up. 'And I'm sick of playing in this stupid sailor town. They don't buy my basketballs. They don't buy my sneakers. I'm bigger than Sam Houston in Texas. I can go into the mayor's office there and sit down in his chair. I want to be traded.'

Eventually, of course, Hayes would manage to transfer the entire team to his college town of Houston. But the headline in the stupid sailor town the next morning scared him. For the moment, his rebellion was doused. Elvin had never talked to me. He didn't even know I was on the trip.

While the players were still sitting around the locker room looking at each other suspiciously, a substitute forward named Toby Kimball, a nice, bald rebounder from the University of Connecticut, finally spoke up. 'Men, I can't let us go through with this,' he said. 'Elvin, I was sitting right behind you and Callahan on the bus. I heard all that stuff: "They don't buy my sneakers, they don't buy my basketballs . . ."'

Tough guy Hannum had to be separated from Hayes. At the noon press conference, Elvin abjectly apologised to the city.

Until Alex filled me in several years later, I didn't know the backstory. So I missed the moral in what happened next.

Toby Kimball was traded to Milwaukee.

AQUA VELVA

Midwestern newspapers weren't in agreement on how to cover the Evansville crash, when the basketball team, the coach, the manager and everyone else aboard died in a small aeroplane that didn't quite lift off from Indiana. Half of the papers dispatched cityside reporters. (The *Chicago Sun-Times* was one of those.) Half, including the *Cincinnati Enquirer*, sent sportswriters. It was pretty interesting.

The cityside reporters hung around the airport interviewing the investigators. The sportswriters hung around the chapel talking to the crying kids, who were stroking one another's hair.

In the morning, both divisions of chroniclers were loaded on a boxcar in a light rain and taken a short way by rail to the muddy crash site on the rim of the airport. The cityside reporters concentrated on the logistics: here was the fuselage, there was the wing. The sportswriters wrote about the Aqua Velva aftershave bottle that didn't break. The salad dressing was unused, the luggage undamaged. Everything survives but the people.

Only the captain was still unaccounted for.

'Did we have an Oriental pilot?' one FAA man called calmly to another.

'Yeah, I think so,' his partner answered in a drowsy voice. 'I got him.' Their colloquy was colder than the rain. But, to the sportswriters, it had a familiar timbre. It reminded them of the grizzled pros in the losing locker rooms holding in their hearts by sticking out their chests, trying not to weep.

A HORN HONKING

A coach who presided over some of the most dramatic events in sports acknowledged off the record that he had epilepsy. But, emphatically, he did not want it written, and it never has been. The information was inadvertently dropped to a writer, who probably would have argued for going public even if it wasn't a story that could have done some good. But the man said no and that was the end of it.

Well, not entirely.

A year or so later, it developed that the coach was a private pilot, prompting the writer to print a blind item, leaving out even the name of the sport, questioning the propriety of epileptic pilots.

The FAA telephoned. When the writer said he had nothing to add, someone on the conference call coyly enquired, 'Does Mr [so-and-so] know?'

'I'm not going to play that game,' the writer said and hung up. But they had the right owner. Shortly after that, the coach quietly stopped piloting. At this point, another call came in to the newspaper office. It was a baseball player, an All-Star, who said he understood the unnamed coach's reticence. 'As much as you want to knock down ignorant misconceptions,' he said, 'you don't want epilepsy to be read into every argument you have with the umpires. I have epilepsy. I don't think it's such a big deal. The day I retire, we'll talk about it.'

And, when that day came, we did.

After a seventh knee operation, Buddy Bell retired from the Texas Rangers in the middle of his 18th season, freezing his odometer at 2,514 hits, some 500 shy of the usual standard for sainthood. His lifetime batting average was .279. He had been picked for five All-Star games. Six times he was anointed the best-fielding third baseman in the American League, where he began his career with Cleveland in 1972.

Two years into that career, at the age of twenty-three, Bell was watching football on television, enjoying the company of a younger brother. 'The next thing I knew,' Buddy said, 'there were paramedics standing over me and my brother looked scared to death. I thought, "God, what's going on here?"'

He wouldn't find out for some time.

'The following summer, I was on the golf course with three teammates – Alan Ashby, Joe Coleman and Ed Crosby. It was a game day; we weren't supposed to be playing golf. When the seizure hit, I fell out of the cart and broke my nose. An ambulance came right onto the fairway – a big scene. It embarrassed the hell out of me. Because I didn't want to get us all into trouble, I didn't say anything at the ballpark that night.

'The first time up, I hit a double. I could hardly run. I could hardly see. I was exhausted.'

For several days afterward, Crosby's eyes avoided Bell's. The horror this signalled helped nudge Buddy to a hospital. 'When I wake up from these things,' he said, 'I don't remember having been out of control. Not knowing what happened can be more frightening than anything. All I feel is exhaustion. It's strange. Your body is totally spent. It's like you've just run ten miles as fast as you can, not that I've ever run ten miles in my life.'

The doctors tapped his spine, photographed his brain, pinched him, poked him and terrified him for a week.

'"What's wrong with me?" I kept saying, first to myself and then out loud.' After four days of sombre glances, one doctor hesitantly replied, 'It might be a tumour.'

Bell lost his breath. 'When finally they said "epilepsy", I thought, "Whoa. Should I be happy or sad?" You've got to understand. I grew up in a not-so-normal atmosphere. I was never a normal kid to begin with. I was always "Gus Bell's boy". All I ever wanted was for people to look at me like anyone else, and now I had epilepsy.'

In his prime, during the 1950s, Gus Bell was one of the

brightest stars of the Cincinnati Reds. Later, in his athletic dotage, he patrolled forlorn outfields for the just-arriving New York Mets and the soon-departing Milwaukee Braves. 'There was a time,' Buddy recalled, 'when I thought everyone's dad was a baseball player. But, however his team was doing, it never disrupted our life at home. He was so consistent. The lesson I got from that was not to dwell on the good or bad.'

Only at his own valedictory did it occur to the son that 'the happiest day of my life', the day Gus retired as a player, 'may have been the saddest day of his. Of course, the way I looked at it, he'd be able to go to my games now. Eventually I came to realise that he would have loved a baseball job. But the ones he was offered wouldn't support seven children. So he sold cars, real estate. I don't ever remember him getting down, though.'

And he did go to Buddy's high school games. To stay out of his son's light, the old ballplayer watched from the car, which was parked so far away it was a wonder he could see anything. 'Every time I did something good,' Buddy recalled, 'I could hear a horn honking in the distance.'

Both of Bell's parents, like all parents, were petrified by the diagnosis. 'But, as soon as we heard that most cases were controllable by medication, we all pulled together,' he said. 'In these kind of things, the people around you pick you up. At first the medicine scared me. Besides making my gums very, very sore, it turned me sort of complacent. I worried whether I could still play. But once I got used to the stuff, it was like waking up and drinking orange juice. Pretty soon I was back on my game.'

Bell said, 'One reason I never wanted people to know was just that I didn't want them to worry about me. I don't think about it every day. I don't think about it every month. I'd be the same way without it.'

His last horrible seizure came in New York City. 'It was my

own dumb fault, I kind of got away from the medication, started to become the doctor. It was the morning before a game. Thank goodness I wasn't anyplace where I could hurt somebody. Afterward, it felt like I'd been run over by a truck. I learned my lesson for good.'

Baseball made him rich. Unlike his father, Buddy could comfortably remain in the game, taking modest personnel jobs until he learned his way back to the big leagues. As the manager of first the Detroit Tigers and then the Colorado Rockies, and finally as a coach back with his original team, the Indians, Buddy especially enjoyed nurturing the youngest talent. His oldest son, David, made it not only to the majors but to the World Series.

Along with Gus, who is gone now, Buddy had watched David's high school games from the car. The father and the grandfather sat together in the front seat, talking about baseball and life.

They contemplated curveballs and the changing seasons.

Now and then, they honked the horn.

I WANT TO THANK MY WIFE'S HUSBAND

Barrelling past Babe Ruth and Roger Maris, Mark McGwire set an even more astonishing record for thank-yous. Speaking into an onfield microphone after hitting home run No. 62, McGwire saluted not only his ex-wife but also her current husband, both present in a cloak of relatives gathered around the St Louis slugger.

This, of course, was a kindness to a ten-year-old boy named Matt, a plump strawberry-blond sporting his own Cardinals uniform with 'McGwire' on the back. One untold detail from a saga that didn't withhold many details was the fact that Matt's hair had been dark when the chase began and would return to a natural colour the following season.

'It's a California thing,' the father shrugged at first, and that's true enough. But there was a little more to it.

Because Matt had his mother's olive skin and dark hair, not to mention a different address and a stepfather, not all of his classmates believed he was Mark McGwire's son. But he needn't have dyed his hair to prove it. Every time Mark stepped on a historic plate, he lifted Matt like a flag and waved him to the world.

JAMES T. FARRELL

The Mets were in the World Series and Willie Mays, on his last swings, was in the batting cage. Throughout the '80s and '90s, every time I heard Joe DiMaggio introduced as 'the greatest living ballplayer', I asked aloud, 'Has Willie Mays died?'

Behind the cage stood a mussed, bespectacled, Burgess Meredith–looking fellow of 65 or 70, who introduced himself as Jim Farrell. While he wore a press credential, he didn't quite pass for a newspaperman. Because he had the easy grace and natural slouch of an athlete, I took him for an old ballplayer. In the course of our conversation, conducted to the rhythm of Willie's bat, it dawned on me who he was.

'You're James T. Farrell,' I said suddenly.

'Don't rub it in,' Farrell replied.

Clumsily then, I muttered absolutely the worst thing I could have muttered, something complimentary about *Studs Lonigan*. Farrell actually cringed. 'I've written a lot of books since then,' he said, not exaggerating. 'If you'd like, I'll send you some.'

In short order, a crate of paperbacks arrived, '30s romances with watercolour covers, the kind that used to be associated with drugstores. 'Every year I write a book,' Farrell wrote in the accompanying note, 'and every year the *New York Times* reviews it. The reviewers' complaint is always the same: that the characters say "swell" instead of "cool". Well, they said "swell" in the '30s.' The postscript read, 'Poor Willie'.

SPARKY

Sparky Anderson's father had just gone into the hospital. 'But he's OK,' Sparky said, 'he had this same thing a few years ago. I'm going to stop off and see him on this coming road trip. Roger's going to manage one game.' Roger Craig, Billy Consolo – all of the Tigers coaches, it seemed – lived on the same patch of suburbia outside Detroit. Earlier that morning, the whole gang had dropped by Anderson's house (Craig in a cowboy hat), partly to plot the game Sparky expected to miss, but mostly to teach a yellow Labrador puppy how to walk.

Consolo and Anderson were kids together in Los Angeles. Billy, the star of the neighbourhood, became a 'Bonus Baby' with the Red Sox. Sparky scratched and scrambled in the minors, ending up playing just one season in the big leagues, with the Philadelphia Phillies. The estimable Dodger manager, Walter Alston, had just one at-bat in the majors. Earl Weaver of the Orioles didn't even have that. But, of all the minor-league players who only dropped in on the show, Anderson had the strangest résumé. He started all 154 games of his only year, playing the keystone corner with Granny Hamner.

On Consolo's and Anderson's earliest sandlot team, Buckwheat of the *Little Rascals* roamed the outfield. The young actor was the only one who arrived at the games in a limousine.

'Buckwheat could neither hit nor field,' Anderson said disgustedly, 'but we were forced to let him play. He had equipment.'

Equipment was always problematic. As a grade school kid, Sparky batboyed at the University of Southern California mostly in pursuit of equipment. 'I'd take a new ball out of the box, tug on the seam a little bit and show it to Coach Rod Dedeaux. "All right," he'd say, "you can have that one. But I hope we don't find too many of those.'"

At the height of his life in crime, Sparky led a late-night raid on bandleader Harry James, who sponsored his own baseball team. 'It's true,' Anderson confessed ruefully, 'we swiped all of Harry James's equipment.' In a kitchen drawer of the old Anderson house, a little chocolate-coloured glove was kept for backyard catches. 'With my grandfather, not my father,' Sparky said. 'My father is a good man, but he was never gentle, not to me. I've seen a little gentleness with the grandkids. He's been a little better with them. But no, he was never gentle with me.'

At that point, the phone rang and Sparky answered it.

'Mama,' he said in despair. 'Oh, Mama. I'm so sorry, Mama.'

What he said next wasn't a lie, not in his heart.

'Mama, he was such a gentle man.'

CAN YOU HEAR THAT?

Baseball's All-Star games all seem to run together. This one may have been in Pittsburgh or it might have been in Kansas City. It was a wet night, I remember that. Batting and infield practice were cancelled. But the underground cage was busy. 'Can you hear that?' Willie Stargell asked, lowering the bat he gripped and twirled at the very nub. In between the cannonade noises exploding from the cage, a muted *kaplunk, kaplunk, kaplunk* was heard. 'What the hell is that?'

Leading a search party of three, Stargell followed the kaplunking through a crevice into the catacombs of the stadium under girders and over debris until he came into a semi-lit opening and burst into laughter.

In the half-light crouched Brooks Robinson, the magnificent

third baseman, throwing a ball up against a cinder block wall, taking infield.

THE DEAD MOTHER'S IN THE OTHER CLUBHOUSE

Earl Weaver always preferred heathens to what he called 'God guys'. He fretted that God guys might decide that losing was God's will. 'Skip, don't you want me to walk with the Lord?' Oriole outfielder Pat Kelly once asked.

'Kel,' replied the manager patiently, 'I'd sooner you walk with the bases loaded.'

Up three games to one in a World Series against Pittsburgh, everything looked perfect for Baltimore. Weaver had a trio of Cy Young Award–winning pitchers lined up and only one more game to play in Pittsburgh. Frankly, the Pirate players were already planning their vacations.

Kiko Garcia was pretty much pencilled in as the Most Valuable Player. It would be Kiko's one chance to be remembered.

But then something happened that almost had to be classified as divine intervention. Chuck Tanner's mother died.

Suddenly the Pirates had a reason to play the fifth game: for their grieving manager. After that, what the fuck, as they would say, they were only one game down. Finally, they were tied.

Defying a commissioner's ruling, doing everything he could think of to get back to the normal routine of the regular season, Weaver smuggled several Baltimore and Washington writers into the closed clubhouse before the seventh game. But he kept telling them over and over, 'I got a bad feeling about this.' After Willie Stargell homered and Pittsburgh won in seven, Weaver was back in his office, where many more writers were lining the walls, when President Carter entered in a phalanx of Secret Servicemen.

'I was very sorry,' Carter told Weaver, 'to hear about your mother.'

For just an instant, you could imagine being present at the biggest news event of the century. But, in one of the upsets of the century, Weaver held his spectacular temper. He diplomatically explained the President's confusion of managers.

Later, when Carter was gone, and all of the reporters' questions had been parried, and everyone was filing out of the office, Weaver sat down at his desk to a paper plate of fried chicken and summed up fate and the Series in a sentence: 'The dead mother is in the other clubhouse, Mr President.'

TAKE THREE DOLLARS

Joe Louis died on a Masters Sunday, the day Tom Watson won his second green jacket. As Watson was running through his birdies and bogeys afterward, I left the pressroom, went to the caddie house and knocked on the door. In those days, all of the caddies at Augusta National, like all of the waiters and all of the shoeshine men, were black.

'Did you hear?' I said. 'Joe Louis died.'

Thousand-year-old men with liquid eyes sat down so they wouldn't fall down, and I entered the tumbledown shanty through a spring-loaded screen door and sat off to the side and didn't say another word as, one by one, they passed around their memories of Louis, of Atlanta, of Moline, of Detroit, of neighbourhood stoops, of radios, of the second Max Schmeling fight and of golf. Eddie Futch, the beautiful trainer who grew up with Louis in Detroit, blamed the first Schmeling fight on golf.

'Once he got a hold of those clubs,' Eddie said, 'you could never get through to him.'

I caddied for Louis once, when I was a boy. That is, I caddied for two pros in his threesome while Joe rode a cart with his wife. The occasion was an all-black tournament in Baltimore sponsored by Ballantine Beer, officially titled 'The Three-Ring Open' but colloquially referred to as 'The Three-Ring Circus'. After just about every hole, Louis dipped into a little black physician's bag his wife guarded and dug out a fistful of cash with bills pointed every whichaway. He extended the bird's nest toward the pros and each one plucked what he was owed.

At the end of the round, Louis asked me, 'What's the charge?'

'Nothing,' I said.

'For attending the pins?'

'I don't charge for that.'

'What do you get per bag?'

'Three dollars.'

He held out that huge fist. 'Take three dollars,' he said, and I did.

By the time I left the Augusta caddie house, it was pitch black, and there was only one other shadow on the walk, and I don't expect anyone to believe this, but it was Ernie Banks.

'Ernie, Ernie, what are you doing here?' I said.

'I'm lost,' said Mr Cub in that deep, loud, wonderful voice of his, tossing an arm around me and laughing. 'I've been trying to find the press headquarters. I'm looking for Bob Verdi of the *Trib*. I hear the writers can play the course tomorrow and I want to see if I can join you guys.'

Oh, Ernie.

ALI'S BOSWELL

Phenomenon, Howard Cosell's most conservative description of himself, hardly began to tell it. A homely Jewish lawyer from Brooklyn – the grand slam of network liabilities – achieved a celebrity so enormous and unlikely that he only naturally mistook it for love. Walking along the avenue, stooped and trembling, Cosell was sung to by construction workers and cops, who offered lifts in their patrol cars when cabs were scarce.

He was the national earache, proclaimed both best and worst by *TV Guide*. 'Howard Cosell,' Jimmy Cannon wrote, 'put on a toupee and changed his name [from Cohen] to tell it like it is.'

Cosell's historic alliance with Muhammad Ali, a boon to both of them, was rooted in constitutional law. Cosell knew the Muslim fighter stood on firm legal ground in conscientiously objecting to the draft. But he also thought Ali was right.

In the second act, the fun went out of hating Howard. The anti-Semitic and the anti-semantic lined up together. Bar patrons bought raffle tickets for the honour of chucking bricks through TV sets when his face came on the screen. Pulling out of arenas, Cosell's limousine was rocked like a deposed dictator's. With characteristic understatement, he said, 'I have been vilified more than Charles Manson.'

Come the final act, he remained peculiar and pedantic but he was no longer passionate, and he no longer aroused passion. Cosell became most comfortable at congressional hearings condemning boxing. Before the end, he also turned against TV.

'The trouble with sports on television,' he had declared when he was at the top of his game, 'is that there aren't enough true experts.'

'Yes, Howard,' Red Smith agreed, 'there's even one fewer than you think.'

THEY JUST FADE AWAY

Like Patton, Woody Hayes slapped a soldier – in Woody's case, the wrong one. He throttled Clemson's Charlie Bauman, who intercepted the ball, instead of Ohio State's Art Schlichter, who passed it. The Buckeyes lost the Gator Bowl, 17–15; and, for going berserk on national television (again), their 65-year-old coach was fired the following day.

Poetically, Hayes's new headquarters was a cramped office in Ohio State's ROTC building, where he lined up his favourite books by elevens on three shelves behind his desk: first string, second string and third string. He was just moving *Future Shock* down the depth chart when a visitor arrived. Woody declined a request to line up 33 years of players the same way, loath to choose between Archie Griffin and Hopalong Cassady, but he would concede, 'It's hard to imagine putting anyone ahead of Jim Parker.' Parker, a guard and tackle, made his name as a pro (and his place in the Hall of Fame) protecting Johnny Unitas in Baltimore.

'We had only two blacks on the team back then,' Hayes said, 'and Jim came to me and asked me why he was starting and the other fellow wasn't. I looked him straight in the eye and said, "Because the powers that be tell me I can have no more than two and start no more than one. Someday, Goddamn it, I'm going to change that."'

I telephoned Parker to see if he remembered their conversation. He remembered even the 'Goddamn it' part. I found Jim at a packaged goods store he operated in Baltimore.

Parker said, 'My second memory of him – Lord, I've got a thousand memories of him – is: one time, I lost $200 of my scholarship money. It was for books and things. But, to be a big man, I changed all of the bills to singles so I could walk around for a little while feeling the wad in my pocket. I lost it at the movies, I swear to God.'

After a reaming that set a record, Woody replaced the $200 out of his own pocket. The NCAA needn't bother to investigate. The statute of limitations is up. At an Ohio synagogue, eulogising Si Burick of the *Dayton Daily News*, I saw

Hayes sitting in the congregation in his yarmulke and said, 'If you asked Woody Hayes, I don't think he'd say Si was a ripper or a rooter. I think he'd say he was fair.'

'That's right!' Woody shouted.

He was dead himself a few days later.

THESE STUPID MEN

'I don't understand why these men do these stupid things,' Washington Redskins owner Jack Kent Cooke said, referring to a defensive lineman, Dexter Manley. 'We have the good Lord endowing them with unusual talent, and they desecrate this talent by doing these absolutely stupid things, taking drugs. These men are making hundreds of thousands of dollars a year. It is completely beyond me why they do it.'

Not to forgive these stupid men whose problems cannot be solved by hundreds of thousands of dollars, but just in an effort to understand this one character, Manley – a name straight out of a morality play – consider in simple terms who he is and exactly what unusual talent was bestowed on him by the good Lord. He is a large black man with a razor slash across his face whose violent abilities were discovered in Houston during a special education class that followed his second try at second grade, when he body-slammed a woman teacher against the blackboard in a rage of frustration and shame. He grew up a chauffeur's son but fleet afoot, too big to be so quick, too gentle to be so mean, too bright to be so ignorant, an unusual talent, all right. Untroubled by the fact that Manley could not read, Oklahoma State presented him with a scholarship and a car. Coach Jimmy Johnson, who followed Manley to Stillwater and effectively closed down the auto show, recalled with amusement the long face on Manley when the new morality was announced. Dexter could always make him laugh.

Manley's college performance earned him only a fifth-round call in the National Football League. The Redskins admired his size and speed. And the disregard he showed for all manner of pain, particularly his own, was very attractive. They lined him up on one flank of the suicide battalion and launched him like a cannonball downfield. When it was discovered that he could speak, Manley became a kind of picaresque celebrity in the nation's capital. He patterned his patter on Muhammad Ali's, but unlike the boxer he had no doctrine. His pronouncements ranged from the intentionally outrageous – 'I'd like to hit Russ Francis in the mouth with a baseball bat' – to the unintentionally frank – 'I said I was going to raise hell on the field and off the field; I haven't let anyone down yet' – to the unbearably fragile – 'I was a mistake, my parents told me. That's why I am the way I am now.'

After each ridiculous scrape with the league and the law, in between alibis too childish for a child, he was capable of tenderness and wisdom. 'I don't have a problem with booze,' he told me. 'I have a problem with living.' He defined life rather well, too. He declared, 'Life is a progress.' He kept confessing over and over, 'I have been a knucklehead.'

Applying his wanton talent to pass-rushing, Manley became a legitimate star. But the Mohawk days of 'Mr D.' began to wane on a Monday night when the New York Giants made a wish with quarterback Joe Theismann's fibula. 'I can recall that so vividly,' Manley told a Senate panel studying illiterate athletes. 'I had so much fear and insecurity.'

This revelation of a life after football pushed him into a reading school for the learning disabled. During Manley's halting testimony, the senators seemed to be holding the weeping ogre in their arms.

The last time I talked to Manley, he was on his way to jail. He didn't have to go. Dexter had been offered probation. But he didn't want any threats hanging over him. 'I don't trust myself,' he said. 'I'm not stupid.'

THE KID

Sometimes you don't have to go looking for a story. Sometimes, like on Christmas night in 1977, you just have to glance up from your paper on the aeroplane to find that the story is sitting beside you.

'Is California your home?' the boy asked.

'No, I'm going out to the Rose Bowl,' I said. 'How about you?'

'I'm going to Santa Anita,' he said, 'to see my Derby horse.'

Now I knew who the boy was.

'What's his name?'

'Affirmed.'

'I thought you were headquartered in New York.'

'Not this winter. A lot of trainers I ride for have a lot of horses at this meet that starts tomorrow. Laz Barrera, the Cuban trainer, is picking me up at the airport. Or his son is. California tracks are harder, faster. I have nine mounts tomorrow. [He would ride four winners.] But I'm especially anxious to get back with Affirmed. Just four months and a few days now. My first Kentucky Derby.'

The flight attendant offered the boy a *Sports Illustrated* that, as she failed to notice, had his picture in pink silks on the cover. He declined the magazine and the meal, saying, 'I better skip the Greek lasagna, huh?'

'Do you worry about height as well as weight?'

'What good would it do? I grew half an inch last year. I'm 5 ft 1½ in. tall I'm 17 years old. I'm hoping I'll only have about six more months of bone growth. But who knows?'

'Do you miss school?'

'I've made closer friends at the racetrack. They're not really close, either. But they're close in a way. We play cards. Racetrack rummy. You can learn more than you can in school.'

He asked, 'Do you know Frank Deford?'

'Yeah, did he write the *SI* piece?'

'He only talked to me about 15 minutes. The rest was all him.'

'He's a good guy.'

'Seemed like it.'

'California is supposed to be a tough racing spot,' I said. 'Seattle Slew didn't care for it, did he?'

'Seattle Slew wasn't allowed to get acclimated. Smog, for one thing. I'm not surprised [trainer] Billy Turner isn't with Slew anymore. Those four people who own the horse drove him crazy. They're nice people. But they're around every morning. That can drive you crazy.'

'Billy liked to drink a little, didn't he?' I said.

'I don't blame him.'

'Everything's always fine if you win.'

'I know it,' he said. 'If a great jockey and a great man like Bill Shoemaker doesn't win every single day, they say he's old. And, around the racetrack, people you remember building someone up just two years ago are tearing them down today. Don't worry, I know why everyone likes me now.'

'Being on the West Coast, you'll probably end up on Johnny Carson's show.'

'Maybe, but it's not a lifelong dream of mine.'

'And that would be the Derby?'

He didn't answer immediately. He thought about it for a moment.

'The greatest thing, greater than the Derby, even – greater than anything – is to be on a fast horse. Not an expensive horse, a fast horse. Some of them are expensive just because of their breeding. It's not the way they look, either. It's how they feel – in the hands.'

'Your hands aren't as big as I thought.'

'No, not big, delicate. To ride a fast horse like Johnny D. or Affirmed is fun. I can't wait to see Affirmed.'

With that, Steve Cauthen leaned back, yawned and went to

sleep. Just four months and a few days later, Affirmed and Cauthen won the Derby. They won the Preakness. They won the Belmont Stakes. Alydar just couldn't catch them. 'Stevie Cauthen is like from another planet,' said Laz Barrera, the Cuban trainer. 'It's like he arrived here on a flying sausage.'

The following year, the Kid went into a horrendous slump. He lost his beloved Affirmed to Laffit Pincay Jr. Around the racetrack, people you remembered building him up started tearing him down. And he didn't stop growing at 17 and a half, as he had hoped. Ultimately he sprouted his way entirely out of American racing and over to Europe, where horsemanship meant more than weight, where the tracks were idiosyncratic and fun. The horses sometimes ran clockwise and sometimes ran counterclockwise. Every course, every race, was unique.

One Wimbledon fortnight, I stopped off at the York track to see Cauthen, and, shaking his still delicate hand, I asked him straight off, 'How are the horses over here?'

He smiled just the way he had at Churchill Downs on the first Saturday in May. 'Some of them,' he said, 'are really fast.'

THE UNICORN

Smoking, drinking and thinking, Ben Hogan sat in the window at Shady Oaks in Fort Worth, looking out at the 18th hole. In a manner of speaking, he was *on* the 18th hole.

Dave Kindred and I approached with trepidation, but Hogan smiled. 'Welcome, welcome,' he said. 'It's nice to have you here. It's good to see you.' ('Soft as a fire hydrant,' Grantland Rice had called him. Not necessarily so.) Dave and I were just back from Carnoustie, where in 1953 Hogan won the only British Open he ever played, along with the Masters, the US Open and, all told, five of the six tournaments he entered that year. (In the sixth, he took third place, the bum.)

We were full of stories about the famous sixth hole at

Carnoustie, a par-5 that the Scots consider a monument to
Ben. But he seemed a little rattled by the subject.

Finally, he said, 'I don't remember individual holes
anymore.' There was an uncomfortable pause. 'That's all right,
Mr Hogan,' we told him. 'They all remember you.'

BETTER NOT MENTION SAM GIANCANA

'Country-club prison' is an easy phrase. But golf isn't actually
available at the Federal Correctional Institution in Wisconsin,
where the former Chairman of the House Ways and Means
Committee, Dan Rostenkowski, was serving 17 months for
mail fraud.

'In the old days in Washington,' Rostenkowski said on the
phone, 'those of us who were really dedicated would head out
at five-thirty, six o'clock in the morning – in the dark, teeing
off at daybreak – to get in 18 at Congressional and still make
it back to the floor for the first roll-call at noon. Oh, geez. Bob
Michel, Tip O'Neill, Marty Russo, Danny Rostenkowski, we
always kept our clubs in the trunk because the locker room
wasn't even open at that hour. The ticks were out then, and
those gnats. Oh, they drove you crazy. It was wonderful.

'I haven't had a club in my hand for a year, but I think of
golf all the time, and Congressional, and Medinah, and Sam
Snead, and Bo Wininger, and everything. Non-partisanship.
Golf is the one place where Democrats and Republicans get
along. Jerry Ford's son's bachelor party was at Congressional,
did you know that?'

Why did Rostenkowski take my call?

'I don't know. I haven't taken any others. I don't relish
interviews now, because of where I am. But you said you
wanted to talk about golf.'

Rostenkowski was in the Congressional gallery that tramped
after Ken Venturi on that historic day of delirium in the 1964

US Open. The chairman was at Medinah in 1975 when Lou Graham won his Open in a play-off with John Mahaffey. So was I. 'Do you remember that terrific electric storm that came up on Saturday?' he asked. 'That lightning bolt at 17?'

'Mostly,' I told him, 'I remember that Sam Giancana was murdered in his basement over the weekend. That was the big story in the Chicago papers.'

'Maybe we better not talk about that,' Rostenkowski said, 'on a tie-line to a penitentiary.'

HIGH STICKING AND LOW TREASON

The cost of a seat in the penalty box was that, every time a puck flew into the crowd, you had to reach under your chair into a bucket of chilled replacements and toss a new biscuit onto the ice. It was great fun.

The seating had been arranged by John Hewig, a stubborn public relations man, who was sick of the annual 'white toothless Canadians' column and decided the problem might be that the writer wasn't close enough to the action.

In the third period (two half-times, no bands), the inevitable fight broke out and a bent-nosed Minnesotan named Dale Smedsmo skated over to the box, enraged. Cursing, he slammed down his stick and threw off his gloves. He sat there, panting and sweating, for almost a full minute before realising he wasn't alone.

Leaning to his left, Smedsmo enquired politely, 'What did they get you for?'

'Treason,' I said. He nodded.

THAT'S BOXING ALL OVER

Don Elbaum, a bulb-nosed promoter from Cleveland, once matched the two worst heavyweights he could find with the understanding that the loser retire. It was, of course, a draw.

To juice up a show at the Felt Forum, Elbaum brought Sugar Ray Robinson back to Madison Square Garden and presented him with the actual gloves from his first Garden fight. Alzheimer's didn't have Robinson completely in its grasp yet. Ray was touched, teary-eyed. He hugged the crusty brown gloves.

'Try 'em on, Ray,' a photographer said. Elbaum tried to wave off the demonstration, but he was too late.

Both gloves were left-handed.

EUGENE AT THE SUPER BOWL

Mercury Morris did the crime. Eugene Morris was doing the time. 'A prison is lit up like a stadium,' he said from the other side of a visiting room table in Florida's Dade County, 'and sometimes it even sounds like a football game. Every team has fans in here [the Miami Dolphins remained Merc's team], and the countdown to the Super Bowl is amazing. For just a normal four o'clock game, they start staking spots at the TV around eleven.' Morris said he always waited for the kick-off and then, as if Bob Griese had just pressed the ball into his stomach, he made a broken-field run to the telephone.

'That's when the line is the shortest,' he said.

THE COWBOY

'A real cowboy,' Reggie Jackson said in his enthusiastic way. 'His word is his bond, his saddle is his ride, his horse is his best friend.' But Gene Autry's horse was long dead and the Angels' singing owner would spend 30 dusty years in baseball without ever finding another Champion. By the time Anaheim would sing in 2002, Gene would be long gone, himself. Near the end of an Autry interview conducted by Jack Murphy, the late

Champion came up along with the old rumour that he had been stuffed. 'I got to be honest with you about that,' Autry said. 'Roy Rogers had Trigger stuffed. I probably should have had Champion stuffed. But a taxidermist came in and gave us an estimate. I believe it was $80,000.

'I said, "Bury the son of a bitch."'

BURIED IN PINK

'This is the one,' said Vitas Gerulaitis, the retiring (but not shy) tennis player turning full throttle to golf. 'This is my baby.'

Rolf Deming, the pro at the Saddlebrook resort in Florida, waggled the club respectfully and was too polite a man and too resourceful a teacher to say it seemed like any other 5-iron to him.

'It's magic,' Vitas proclaimed, and everyone grinned.

We played 36 holes that day. Gerulaitis drove the cart like Gene Hackman under the el trains, as though Vitas were in a frenzied hurry to become as good at golf as he had been at tennis.

Just a few weeks later, Gerulaitis died in a manner almost too awful to tell. In perfect health, he lay down for a nap in a friend's pool house and expired of the carbon monoxide poison seeping from a faulty heater.

He was buried with his favourite . . . well, the obituary in the *New York Times* should have read 'Ping 5-iron'. But a copy editor must have thought he (or she) knew better, or perhaps it was just an old-fashioned typographical error. In any case, for the rest of time, the paper of record buried Vitas Gerulaitis 'with his favourite pink 5-iron'.

Does it get any crueller than that?

Lost in the Fog of Time

As a breed of men, sportswriters are not especially steady on their feet, particularly after dinner. Teetering home from a Christmas party, Kenny Jones of *The Independent* in London fell onto the Underground tracks and a train took off his right hand.

A Welshman (by Richard Burton out of Dylan Thomas), Kenny once had been a professional soccer player. His brother was a star. Almost the first person who telephoned Jones in the hospital was a marvellous old soccer coach named Malcolm Allison. (Kenny told me the story when I called.)

Right off the bat, Allison asked Jones, 'Why do you think the Chinese are so good at table tennis?'

'Beats the bloody hell out of me, Malcolm,' Kenny replied, 'but thanks for bringing that up.'

'It's because they have great touch,' Allison continued, undaunted. 'Do you know why they have great touch?'

'No, Malcolm.'

'It's because they eat with chopsticks.'

Kenny told me, 'I hung up and immediately called Kathleen, and said, "Quick, bring me some chopsticks!" She must have thought I was daft.' He went straight to work.

'I'm already learning to write with my left hand,' he said. 'In our game, you need to, eh?'

He was OK.

'We have a tendency to live in the past,' Jimmy Cannon said for most sportswriters, the males, anyway, 'to let time telescope on us. We live through so many generations of ballplayers that they all get mixed up in our minds. We do not judge time at all. A sportswriter is entombed in a prolonged boyhood.'

In *No Cheering in the Press Box*, Cannon pinpointed for Jerry Holtzman the precise moment Jimmy realised he had grown old:

'I was on the train one day with Mickey Mantle and Whitey Ford. I was telling some Lefty Gomez stories, and Mantle looked at me with amazement. It was his first year. He was about 18 or 19, and he asked, "Did you see Gomez pitch?"

'Did I see Gomez pitch? I travelled with the ball club when he was pitching. He was my running mate on the road. Mantle looked at me with great astonishment, and the thing that hit me was that Gomez was about the same age as I am. And I realised he was being regarded by Mantle the same way I used to listen to Damon Runyon and Warren Brown talk about guys like Moose McCormick and Amos Rusie. They were just some guys lost in the fog of time.'

Jim Palmer is about the same age as I am. Just a couple of months separate us. In early days at the *Baltimore Evening Sun*, I was momentarily furloughed from the tennis, swimming, boxing and high school beats, not just casually invited to write about Palmer but specifically assigned to write him off. The 20-year-old star of the 1966 World Series, the last pitcher to beat Sandy Koufax, was sore-armed and evidently washed up with the Orioles at 22. Palmer wasn't even going to spring training with the big club. He was already consigned to the bushes of Miami, Elmira and Rochester.

Wanting to stop by the Department of Motor Vehicles that morning before making his way to the minor-league camp, Palmer asked if we could do the interview at the *Sun* office downtown. During all of his time in Baltimore, he had neglected to acquire a Maryland driver's licence. The traffic officer who eventually stopped him graciously accepted his celebrity licence. But, realistically, Palmer decided he'd better not depend on that much longer.

Striding into the newsroom, Palmer took a seat amidst a cluster of desks and a clatter of deadlines and began telling his story. 'I'm not washed up,' he said. 'They're just punishing me because they think I'm a hypochondriac. I'm going to be the best pitcher in the American League. As a matter of fact, I *am* the best pitcher in the American League.'

Palmer recapped his elbow miseries, starting with his first shot of cortisone. 'It's a tremendous drug,' he said, 'for a week.' After shutting out and almost no-hitting the New York Yankees on a frosty day in May, he had been unable to lift his arm for the next turn. Palmer said, 'Cat knows what it feels like,' referring to the Orioles pitching coach Harry 'The Cat' Brecheen. 'But everyone else thinks it's in my head. I mean, logically, at my age, why wouldn't you want to pitch? We have a good-offence, good-defence ballclub, and I don't want to pitch? I could see a fringe pitcher hanging on that way, but not me. You get paid on your record. When I was fifteen-and-ten and the biggest winner on the staff, [general manager] Harry Dalton said, "You were only five games over five hundred." So, you can see where the player stands.'

Palmer was certainly a hypochondriac, but he was also hurt. 'They're just gypping me out of pension money,' he said. 'Last year, they gave me their word I'd go down to the minors for the minimum stay, and if my arm hurt at all, they'd bring me back and put me on the disabled list. They put me on the DL, all right. Rochester's. That cost me 90 days' pension time right there. It's all just bullshit and money. All of the bullshit and all of the money have nothing to do with what baseball is.'

'What is baseball?' I asked him.

'Baseball,' he said, 'is romance.'

Of course, following his stretch in exile, Palmer went on to have a long career, to pitch more than 200 complete games with that washed-up arm, to be the best pitcher in the American League, to win a wallful of Cy Young Awards, to become synonymous with the Orioles, to pose for underwear ads, to make the Hall of Fame, to attempt a post-Cooperstown comeback and to pitch expensive loans to bad credit risks on television.

Through it all, the Orioles never did cure the hypochondriac. 'Fuck his Goddamned ulna nerve,' Earl Weaver said medically. 'That fuckin' Palmer worries about the fuckin' line his fuckin' cap leaves on his fuckin' forehead.'

Just as unscientifically, I've drawn an odd line of comfort from Palmer's enduring presence on the stage and his Dick Clarkian youthfulness. Often I turn around and Palmer's there.

Once I turned around and Koufax was there.

It was spring training and I was at Vero Beach to see Orel Hershiser for a *Time* cover story I was writing on Doc Gooden. Si Burick of the *Dayton Daily News* had just died – I delivered one of the eulogies – and a couple of us were talking about him.

'Excuse me,' Koufax said, tugging at my elbow. 'Did I hear you say Si Burick died?'

'Yes,' I said. 'I just came from the funeral.'

'Aw,' Koufax said. 'I loved Si.'

While almost everyone loved Si, this was still startling. Koufax didn't mourn the passing of too many sportswriters.

Standing there in his Dodgers' '32', even with his pewter hair peeking out from under the cap, Koufax looked ready to pitch. He was about the same age as I am now. After exchanging Burick stories, and laughing sadly, we discussed Gooden, Hershiser, Bret Saberhagen, Roger Clemens, Tom Browning and a few other pitchers on my list. I filled him in on everything Don Drysdale had told me the day before in Sarasota. 'He kept mentioning you,' I told Koufax, 'and saying, "Let's see Gooden do it for five straight years, like Sandy."' Koufax smiled.

Finally, I introduced myself, and his face dropped.

'I would never have talked with you if I knew you were from *Time*,' he said.

'Let's pretend we didn't talk then,' I said, probably a little harshly.

'No, no, I'm sorry,' Koufax said, grabbing my arm. 'Don't be that way. Please. I'm sorry. Go ahead and use anything I told you, whatever you want. It's just that, years ago, I swore I'd never talk to *Time* or *Sports Illustrated* ever again. They double-crossed me once.'

In his *Farewell to Sport*, Paul Gallico wrote:

'The sportswriter has few if any heroes. We create many because it is our business to do so, but we do not believe in them. We know them too well. We are as concerned as often, sometimes, with keeping them and their weaknesses and peccadilloes out of the paper as we are with putting them in. We see them with their hair down in the locker rooms, dressing rooms, or their homes. Frequently we come quite unawares upon little meannesses. When they fall from grace, we are usually the first to know it, and when their patience is tried, it is generally to us that they are rude and ill-tempered. We sing of their muscles, their courage, their gameness and their skill because it seems to amuse readers and sell papers, but we rarely consider them as people and, strictly speaking, leave their characters alone because that is dangerous ground.'

Some sportswriters, as Koufax apparently discovered, are

dishonest. Not all of the dishonest ones, surprisingly, are looking for a competitive edge. Some would gladly share the improved or invented quote with all of the other writers sitting around them in the press box. They can't help themselves. They just have to make it a little better than it is. They are pathological.

One of the best of this strange breed operated on the outskirts of Baltimore, near enough to the Orioles to become intimate with the players, far enough away not to have to be concerned about too many of them poring over every word he wrote.

In the clubhouse before an Oriole game, I was chatting with a left-field platooner named John Lowenstein when the fabulist interrupted to ask just one question. As usual, it was a deep subject.

'That's a very good question,' Lowenstein said, 'and I can't answer it right this minute, off the top of my head. But, long about 11 o'clock this evening, when you're up there writing in that press box, if you can think of a really good answer, you may quote me.'

The writer moved on, seemingly unaware of what had just taken place.

'So you know,' I told Lowenstein.

'I can read,' he said.

As Mantle came in with Cannon, he went out with us. For that matter, Cannon went out with us. The last time I saw Jimmy, just before the stroke and the wheelchair, a little more than a couple of years before the end, he was exhaustedly climbing onto a press bus at a Super Bowl. Barely 60, Joan Blondell's old lover seemed much older. He was Carol Channing's old lover, too. Occasionally babysitting Frank Sinatra Jr, Jimmy lived a theatrical life.

A family of four – a mother, father, daughter and son – spun past the bus on bicycles. 'Isn't it sad,' said Cannon, who spoke in epigrams, 'what the energy crisis has done to the Hell's Angels?'

Mantle, for whom laziness was something of an art form, carried around a small black electronic box, about the size of a transistor radio, that did a good deal of his cursing for him. Mickey said he found it especially handy on the golf course. 'It's like having Billy Martin in your pocket,' he said. 'Goddamn son of a bitch,' the box said.

At an All-Star game luncheon, after retelling first his staple story of Martin shooting a farmer's cows, followed up by Mickey's famous recurring dream (a little too pat to be believed entirely) of being in uniform but unable to find the entrance to Yankee Stadium as the loudspeaker keeps calling him to bat, Mantle turned to the unprepared text and his embarrassing All-Star record.

'All-Star games were mostly cocktail parties to me and Whitey,' he admitted, 'especially that last game in Anaheim.' Flashing an Oklahoma grin but unable to sustain it, he said, 'I flew in from Dallas that morning and showed up a little hammered just a few minutes before the start. I missed the team photo. Dressing as fast as I could, I pinch-hit in the first inning, struck out on three pitches, helicoptered straight to the airport, flew right back to Dallas, walked into the clubhouse at Preston Trail, looked up at the TV set and saw the game was still going on. I stood there and watched Tony Perez hit a homer in the 15th to win it for the National League. I'm damned ashamed of that.'

The Mick died relatively young, full of regret. Near the end, he looked into a TV camera and spoke directly to America's children. 'I'm a role model, all right,' he told them. 'Don't be like me.'

Old baseball writers used to feel sorry for young ones, who missed the trains. Now I know what they meant. One year at Indy, A.J. Foyt wetted a red bandanna and tied it around his face before he climbed into the car. The next year, watching him pull on a fireproof cowl, I was glad I hadn't missed the bandanna.

Especially at the greatest occasions, sportswriters have multiplied to the point of crowding themselves out of the circle. At the World Series, the batting cage is actually roped off these days, like an exclusive restaurant. Very little space is left in the dugout for sitting with a notebook and trying to pry a column out of Yogi Berra.

For years, I subscribed to the widespread theory that Berra's old St Louis playmate, Joe Garagiola, ghosted most of the funny things Yogi had to say. ('Should I cut this into four pieces or eight pieces?' the pizza man asked. 'Four pieces,' Yogi said. 'I can't eat eight pieces.') Unfailingly, I found the old Yankee catcher to be sweet and slow and terribly dull. Until finally one time, putting my notebook away, I made some light exit conversation: 'When the Mets fired you, Yogi, did you expect to end up back with the Yankees?'

'Yeah, I read in the paper that Billy wanted me back as a coach. But baseball was pretty far from my mind at that moment. That was my first break from the game, really, since I was small. For once, I didn't want to think about baseball. Baseball was the last thing I wanted to think about. I loaded up my kids in the car. I wanted to get as far away from baseball as I could.'

'Where did you go?' I asked.

'The Hall of Fame,' he said.

Frequently we come quite unawares upon little kindnesses.

Sparky Anderson and I had an ugly shouting match at a World Series, having to do with some scepticism I had expressed about the nice but overrated fastball pitcher Don Gullett. That was Sparky's boy. Steam was still coming off both of us at the baseball winter meetings in Hawaii. After a week chained to the lobby, running down false rumours, I went to the Reds' president, Bob Howsam, and asked him, man to man, if he was going to make a big trade or not. Because if he wasn't, I was going to play golf.

'If I do make a deal,' he said, 'it'll only involve a minor-leaguer.'

'Let's be sure we understand each other,' I told him. 'If I play golf and you make a big trade, I'll miss every edition.'

'Our starting eight is set.'

'And pitchers?'

'The only guy we're talking about trading is a minor-leaguer.'

'OK,' I said. 'I'm playing golf.'

On the elevator to the lobby with my clubs on my shoulder, I encountered Anderson. We nodded at each other coldly.

When we reached the lobby, he asked suddenly, 'Where are you going? To play golf?'

'Sparky,' I said, 'that's why you're the Manager of the Year. You see me leaving the hotel with my golf clubs on my back and right away you put it together that I'm on my way to the golf course. Well done.'

I was horrible.

He let me go all of the way out the door. I would have let me go all of the way to the 18th hole. But then he came running outside to grab me.

'Tom,' he said. 'Don't play golf.'

A couple of hours later, Howsam traded minor-league first baseman Dave Revering and $1.7 million for Oakland A's pitcher Vida Blue. An hour after that, commissioner Bowie Kuhn voided the trade and all hell broke loose.

Thanks, Sparky.

Football players were never so accessible, but some years ago, when the Super Bowl grew to an obscene size, something remarkable happened. Early in the week, because of the media crush, the players were moved out of the locker room into a hotel ballroom, where each one met the press at his own table. Perhaps it was the tablecloth that demanded a certain decorum, but the same linebacker who wouldn't stop scratching himself at his locker actually extended his hand across the tablecloth. The writers were the barbarians.

'I'm having trouble keeping this straight,' Trenton's Bus Saidt, a newspaperman right out of *The Front Page*, asked Raiders quarterback Jim Plunkett. 'Is it dead father, blind mother, or dead mother, blind father?'

There was a table-wide gasp, after which the quarterback replied evenly, 'Both of my parents were blind and my mother is dead.'

If that was one of the worst questions ever asked, a candidate for the best one was put to trainer Jack Van Berg a couple of mornings before a Kentucky Derby. His horse, Gate Dancer (who would win the Preakness), was a talented but wild colt whose skittish reaction to loud noises compelled him to wear earmuffs. Gate Dancer had finished first in the Blue Grass Stakes the week before the Derby, but for savaging another horse in the stretch he was dropped to second by the stewards.

'Jack,' someone in the irregular press corps enquired thoughtfully, 'do you think it was discouraging to Gate Dancer to be taken down in the Blue Grass?'

Van Berg looked blankly at the questioner for a lengthy moment and then around at all of the other baseball writers with borrowed binoculars.

'I can't swear to it,' he said finally, 'but I'm pretty sure the horse still thinks he won.'

I haven't been a very successful gambler through the years, but I had a small part once in picking a long shot in San Diego.

A boy from Syracuse, Frank Hamblen, showed up at the offices of the NBA's San Diego Rockets, volunteering to do any job for any amount of money, or no money at all, if he could take a postgraduate course in basketball under the legendary teacher Pete Newell. Newell took a shine to Hamblen and was impressed by him. The Rockets owned the second pick in that year's draft and there were a lot of bushes to beat. Newell not only tutored Frank in the game, but sent him around to the lesser places to inspect the more obscure talent. Pete personally scouted the likely prospects, eventually selecting Rudy Tomjanovich, Calvin Murphy, Mike Newlin . . .

After the Rockets took their turn in the seventh round, by which time any player with a realistic hope of making any team was long gone, Newell turned to Hamblen and said, 'Frank, you make the eighth pick.'

A minute later, we bumped in the hallway. Frank was in a controlled panic. All of the seniors he knew were gone. Feverishly, in a room next to the one where the conference call was in progress, Hamblen and I flipped through a *Street & Smith* basketball magazine searching for a likely name, any likely name. Obviously, it had to be someone who played for a school Frank had seen. Well, he had seen Northwestern.

The Wildcats had a forward who was tall enough, 6 ft 8 in., named Adams, who scored pitifully few points but registered his share of rebounds. Hamblen had no memory of him at all. Frank had been grading players on the opposition.

In the eighth round, the San Diego Rockets selected Don Adams of Northwestern University.

On the morning the rookies mustered, Frank and I were more than a little anxious to see Adams. We didn't even know what colour he was.

He was black.

Into the San Diego Sports Arena slouched a tall black man who had a pathetic fringe of hair around a shiny bald pate and a little potbelly. He looked to be about 50 years old. Frank and I glanced at each other sideways. 'Don Adams,' we both said.

Following their physicals, the players went to lunch. Most of them had a hamburger. Adams had a martini.

And do you know what? He was a hell of a player. He couldn't make any kind of outside shot, but he was an intelligent man who truly understood the game, who never broke the wrong way or threw the wrong pass. And he logged more than his share of rebounds. Adams not only made the team but beat Rudy T. to the starting line-up. Don went on to play for Detroit and Atlanta as well. Wherever he played, he always dropped by the press table and said hello.

I got to thinking of him as Shaquille O'Neal and Kobe Bryant were stringing their three titles in Los Angeles. Sitting beside Phil Jackson on the Lakers' bench was one of his assistant coaches, Frank Hamblen, an NBA champion.

When it came to being in the vicinity of dramatic events, the best sportswriter I ever knew was Sam Lacy of the *Washington* and *Baltimore Afro-American*. Not long before Sam died in 2003, I visited him in his office on Charles Street in Baltimore.

'Can I show you another column I'm working on?' he asked, rising painstakingly and walking slowly to an adjoining room. 'Don't ever grow old, Tom,' Sam said from almost 100 years' experience. 'No,' he changed his mind, 'do.'

After caddieing for the winner in the US Open, 16-year-old Lacy stood by Jim Barnes's bag and watched President Warren G. Harding come onto the 18th green to greet Long Jim.

One of golf's forgotten greats, Barnes had claimed the first two PGA Championships, on each side of the timeout taken for the First World War, and now he had captured the '21 US Open. He would go on to win the '25 British Open. Lacy would go on, too.

Sam's story, which unwinds like an unbroken streamer tossed from the deck of the *Lusitania*, more properly begins in 1913, when he was nine. For that matter, maybe it should start with his grandfather, the first black detective on the District of

Columbia police force, from whom Lacy inherited his knack for being in the hot spot.

At nine, anyway, Sam – Sammy, back then – was shagging baseballs with the rest of the neighbourhood children who haunted Griffith Stadium, home of the Nats. In the hours leading up to the games, he would wrangle messages for the players, pick up Joe Judge's and Goose Goslin's laundry, and play catch with Chick Gandil. Chick was the team's first baseman and Lacy's particular hero, who sometimes sent him with a note to buy cigarettes.

Come the close of that decade, in an Illinois courtroom, Chick would be called Charles Arnold Gandil. By then he was one of the eight Chicago 'Black Sox' players being thrown out of baseball for dumping the 1919 World Series. Sammy listened to the accounts on the radio and sobbed.

Lacy got to the Open on a whim. When his older brother jumped off the streetcar at their regular stop, Sam stayed on all the way to the Columbia Country Club, hoping for a loop with any run-of-the-mill pro but ready to settle for just a glimpse of Walter Hagen. 'That was my favourite golfer,' he said. 'I loved Hagen. He was the dress-up guy among the golfers. I was the dress-up guy among the caddies.'

The most coveted bags belonged to Hagen, Gene Sarazen, Bobby Jones, Bobby Cruickshank, Jock Hutchison and Fred McLeod, but Sam was more than delighted to have snared Barnes, who eight years earlier had finished fourth in the Open behind Francis Ouimet, Harry Vardon and Ted Ray. That nickname, Long Jim, was no lie.

'Columbia had an elevated first tee and a long carry to the fairway,' Sam recalled. 'The caddies would go down early to the landing area.' When Barnes's first drive whistled past, Sam whistled, too.

'Long Jim would say, "Son, how far do we have to go?" And I'd say, "Two hundred yards, sir." And he'd take out a mashie-niblick [seven-iron], not a mashie [five-iron], a mashie-niblick, and I'd just shake my head. Jim was slow-going, easy. A pretty good putter, but he didn't have to be that week. I wouldn't say he was superb around the greens, like Mickelson or Tiger. But he was pretty handy. We won by nine strokes.'

Hagen tied for second. Barnes gave his caddie $200 of the $500 first prize. 'Two fifties and five twenties,' Sam said. 'I had to do some serious explaining to my mother.'

Growing up, as you might imagine, Lacy played more baseball than golf. Knocking around semi-pro ball on the edges of the Negro Leagues, he knew Cool Papa Bell, Oscar Charleston and Biz Mackey, who taught Roy Campanella how to catch. Sam saw Buck Leonard play, and Josh Gibson. He saw a lot more than that.

Sam and Jackie Robinson held back the loose boards for each other so they could slip into ballparks through the outfield fence. One time, in Macon, Georgia, Sam and Jackie stood together on a boarding-house porch as a cross burned white-hot in the front yard.

Because certain kinds of ignorance make a man hungry for knowledge, Lacy quit baseball for Howard University. Then a part-time writing job (a nickel an inch) diverted him and his degree in education away from teaching or coaching and toward the newspaper business: the black papers. Sam's career with them can only be called a quest.

For a while in the early '40s, he traded himself from the *Afro-American* to the *Chicago Defender*, just so he could get in the face of the baseball commissioner, Judge Kenesaw Mountain Landis. When the colour barrier finally fell, Sam was 42 – Jackie's uniform number.

Back at the *Afro-American*, sports editor Lacy accompanied Althea Gibson to her first tennis tournament and brought his readers along. In a manner of speaking, he ran with Olympian Wilma Rudolph in Rome.

When 'Black is beautiful' became a clarion call in America, Lacy wrote, 'An orchid is more beautiful. It's multicoloured, like you and I.'

Not that he didn't encounter the customary slights. Once, introduced at a sportswriters' dinner as 'the boy from the *Afro-American*', Sam rose and said pleasantly, 'I'm the oldest sportswriter here. I'm just wondering, if you could tell me, when will I grow up to be a man?'

Thinking back on all of the years that his wife, Barbara, sat in the Jim Crow section of the bleachers, while Sam sat on the press box roof, he preferred to remember the few white sportswriters who climbed up to join him. They told him they wanted a tan.

But he knew they were lying. 'They had just come from Florida,' he whispered, eyes glistening.

In 1998, when Lacy was inducted into the Baseball Hall of Fame in Cooperstown, he remembered these men in his speech. Sam is in the writers' wing, but not so far from Cool Papa, not so far at all from Jackie.

'Would you tolerate the company of Pete Rose?' I asked.

'Yes, I'm all for tolerance,' he said.

That day of my visit Sam had just finished a column on Kultida Woods: 'There she stood in front of the gallery at every crucial hole, dressed in smiling pink, a feminine component of the perpetual red her son wears when at work. Dad gave him the tough hide of a Vietnam veteran. But Mom instilled Tiger's unflappable grace.'

The picture of unflappable grace, Lacy wore a dapper brown suit (he was the dress-up guy among the sportswriters). His mother, a full-blooded Shinnecock Indian, always showed in his face. But now that he was so thin, she was carved there in light wood, the colour of white coffee. Barbara's wedding ring spun on Sam's bony finger, but it was still there. She died in 1969.

That other column he had gone to find was on cyclist Lance Armstrong. 'For shame that it is taking me so long to write about him,' Lacy said. Of course, Sam's readers were especially interested in Tiger and tennis's Williams sisters. 'Earl Woods and Richard Williams,' Sam said, 'represent the very fathers that are so rare in our world.' But Sam was interested in everything. 'Should I be more concerned with Frank Robinson than Brooks Robinson? The essence of journalism, in my opinion, is just a little restlessness and curiosity.'

When Serena and Venus won the US Open and Wimbledon, like everyone else in the business, Sam tried to reach Althea Gibson. She answered no one but him.

'Sam, it's Althea,' breathed the sad voice on his answering machine. 'I don't have anything to say about tennis anymore.' What Sam and I heard was, 'I don't have anything to say about anything anymore.' He told me, 'I think I know what it is, but I'm going to respect her silence.'

By this time Sam was reporting to his office only on Mondays, usually leaving Washington about 4 a.m. for the 45-mile drive to Baltimore. For several years, since 24 August 1999, the day Sam gave up his car, son Tony had done the driving.

'Did I tell you?' Sam said. 'I had a mild stroke. Quite an experience. It was raining. As soon as I hit the Beltway, the drizzle became a downpour. Lightning. Everything. I was in the far left lane when, oh Lord, the stroke hit me. One lane at a time, I carefully moved over. Eighteen-wheelers came up all around me and sandwiched me in. But somehow I ended up behind one of them and he led me out. The good Lord was at the wheel.'

Written longhand in a hospital bed, Sam's last column appeared on 9 May 2003, the morning after he died. He wrote about an eight-year-old boy named Khari, 'a bundle of energy who shares the apartment next door. He is an excellent student, but like most boys his age, Khari is a fanatic about sports.' Sam also wrote about Khari's mom, Theresa, a strong woman who had what he called a 'take no tea for the fever' attitude. 'In recent months, my 99 years of independence has needed a little help. Some of my missteps have resulted in me winding up on my butt. Enter Theresa. I thought there was no way this woman was going to get me off the floor. Boy, was I wrong. She had me sailing through the air so fast that I thought about taking out flight insurance.'

Reading Sam's column, I remembered the boy who cried for Chick Gandil in 1920, and I thought of Khari, who must have cried, too, but whose hero never let him down.

Near the end of his *Farewell to Sport*, Gallico tried to look ahead. Writing in 1937, he predicted, 'There will appear again within the next 50 years a mighty batter with a deadly eye, and he will hit more home runs than Babe Ruth, and Ruth, the greatest of his age today in baseball, will have become simply a measuring stick, somebody, as a Brooklynite would put it, that somebody else hit more home runs than.'

Ten years after that, in 1947, E.B. White actually foresaw little dirigibles hovering over the stadiums and large television screens blinking in the end zones: 'High in the blue sky above the Bowl, skywriters will be at work writing the scores of other major and minor sporting contests, weaving an interminable record of victory and defeat, and using the new high-visibility pink news-smoke perfected by Pepsi-Cola engineers. And in the frames of the giant video sets, just behind the goal posts, a fan could watch Dejected win the Futurity before a record-breaking crowd of 349,872 at Belmont, each of whom will be tuned to the Yale Bowl and following the World Series game in the video and searching the sky for further news of events either under way or just completed. The effect of this vast cyclorama of sport will be to divide the spectator's attention, over-subtilise his appreciation and deaden his passion.'

In a similar spirit now, one can imagine future basketball players, already the most tattooed body of men outside of the Merchant Marines, pooling their decorations to present small dramatisations as they go, kaleidoscopic theatricals that would fluctuate according to who makes the outlet pass and who fills the lane and depending on the particular way the players weave in and out of their half-court offences. Naturally, personnel would have to shift from team to team even more maniacally than it does now, and how much demand a player is in would depend largely on the versatility of his ink.

The safest forecast of all is that television's hold on sports will increase. In the final college football game of the twentieth century, the winning coach, Florida State's Bobby Bowden, was interviewed by television even as the game went on over his shoulder. The star of the contest, Peter Warrick, earned his school a multimillion-dollar payday just a few weeks after being caught stealing $400 worth of shirts.

Televising that sixty-minute game took over four hours. Fifty years from now, it may take a full day, if not a full week, and the coaches might handle the play-by-play themselves, assisted only by the entire cast of *Saturday Night Live*.

And, for all the bullshit and all the money, as Jim Palmer would probably still say, the games will remain a romance.

Thumbing back through these pages, I notice a monotony of laughter. Ali is having a great laugh. Bird is having a quiet laugh. Koufax is having a sad laugh. There seems to have been an awful lot of laughter.

But that's the memory.

AFTERWORD

The Brick

One year at the British Open, when the tournament was in Sandwich, England, I bed-and-breakfasted with a family in Canterbury. The man of the house was a silent brickmaker who didn't seem to own any shirts. He was constructed of his own hard clay. His wife and mother, who talked more than enough for the three of them, prepared the breakfasts.

Each evening, after the long drive home from Royal St George's, I would dictate my column over a telephone in the foyer. As soon as I got the operator, the brickmaker would come out of his room, take a seat in the shadowy hallway and quietly listen. When I finished, he would go back to bed without comment.

'Do you like golf?' I asked him one morning.

'On television,' he said.

'You've never been to the tournaments?'

'That's for millionaires.'

'No, it's not,' I told him. 'Find yourself a shirt. We're going Sunday.'

At an athlete's pace, with fresh eyes, the broad-backed

strongman followed Jack Nicklaus every stride of the final round. Afterward, I introduced him to Nicklaus, who wasn't just gracious but kind. It hadn't been Jack's happiest week. Back home in Columbus, Ohio, one of his teenage sons, the especially lovable one who didn't always go along with the programme, had rolled the company station wagon – on Jack Nicklaus Freeway! – and been tagged with a DWI. Nobody was hurt, to Jack's immense relief. But he was a father that week, not a golfer. And the few minutes he gave the brickmaker were part of the clearing gentleness that follows the emergency.

Monday morning, as I was packing to leave, my host came to say goodbye. He was shirtless again. 'I know what you do,' he said gruffly. 'Here's what I do.' He handed me an ordinary – that is to say, unextraordinary – but sharply cornered and perfectly rectangular red brick.

'I make bricks,' he said.

He wondered, and I wondered, why I was crying.

But, oh, to be able to make something as substantial and essential as a brick.

Index